CHARLES DICKENS

1812~1870

An Anthology

Engraving by Daniel Maclise, used as the frontispiece to *The Life and Adventures of Nicholas Nickleby* (London, Chapman and Hall, 1839).

CHARLES DICKENS

1812-1870
An Anthology

Chosen and annotated by Lola L. Szladits
from materials in the Berg Collection
of English and American Literature
in commemoration of
the centennial of Dickens's death

The New York Public Library
Astor, Lenox and Tilden
Foundations

Arno Press
A Publishing and Library Service
of The New York Times

Designed and set by Browning Editorial Services, New York, N. Y.

INTRODUCTION

When at ten minutes past six on the evening of Thursday, the 9th of June, 1870, Charles Dickens stopped breathing, the entire world began to mourn. Although he "emphatically" directed that his burial be conducted in an "inexpensive, unostentatious, and strictly private manner" and asked to be buried at the foot of Rochester Castle, in the Kentish countryside he loved and immortalized, the nation claimed him, and buried him in Westminster Abbey. Until the burial on June 16th an endless procession filed past the open grave covering it with flowers and tears. Dickens's wish was carried out in the simple inscription of his name — "without the addition of 'Mr.' or 'Esquire' " — with birth and death dates on the slab stone. Facing it in the Poets' Corner are the monuments of Chaucer, Shakespeare, and Dryden.

A century after Dickens's death, although the "Dickens I Knew" books have subsided, the critical studies, editions of letters, biographical studies, and paperback editions of his novels are still being published in a steady flow. Such works as *Dickens and Crime*, *Dickens and Education*, *Dickens and Kafka*, place Dickens firmly in the twentieth century. G. K. Chesterton wrote: "I am more and more convinced that Dickens will increasingly detach himself from his century, like a mountain from a landscape as we leave it behind." George Orwell, who opened his famous essay with "Dickens is one of those writers who are well worth stealing," pointed out that "the Marxist claims him as 'almost' a Marxist, the Catholic claims him as 'almost' a Catholic, and both claim him as a champion of the proletariat (or 'the poor', as Chesterton would have put it)." As one watches Dickens "detach himself from his century" one retains vividly in one's mind the Kentish countryside — the Pickwick country, as the devotees would have it —, the description of London which, during his endless walks through its streets, furnished the novelist with background for *Oliver Twist* and *David Copperfield*, and that colorful string of characters who came to life in the pages of his books and through his voice on the stage. Dickens has been criticized as a storyteller, but never as a creator of characters. Thackeray begged him not to kill Little Nell and news of her death was awaited in the harbor of New York with the rapt eagerness of a living news item.

When "the Inimitable" himself arrived on these shores, on two different occasions, he was given an emotional welcome. The visit in 1842, at the age of thirty, was memorable because of what Dickens called the "copyright agitation," and he made himself unpopular. His journey also brought out in him the social agitator. He spoke against slavery, visited courts of law, asylums, and prisons, and approved heartily of State support for institutions. But mostly he campaigned for just copyright laws. He had such distinguished American authors on his side as Washington Irving, William Hickling Prescott, William Cullen Bryant, Fitz-Greene Halleck, and Richard Henry Dana.

Dickens's second visit to America was of a different kind. In 1867, already an ailing man, Dickens undertook a sensational reading tour. Lured partly by golden prophecies of fantastic earnings, Dickens gave 423 readings which brought him an estimated total income of £45,000. Wherever he went, New York, Boston, Philadelphia, Baltimore, and Washington — where the President, the Cabinet, and the Supreme Court came to hear him almost in a body —, Dickens was greeted with a frenzy of enthusiasm. He himself exhibited his irrepressible energy by entering into the spirit of such frolics as the Great International Walking Match. This time he also said what his audience wanted to hear. In his farewell address in New York he declared that "if I know anything of my countrymen . . . the English heart is stirred by the fluttering of those Stars and Stripes as it is stirred by no other flag that flies except its own."

It is fitting that The New York Public Library should honor the memory of Charles Dickens. It houses in its Berg Collection of English and American Literature one of the most extensive and best known collections of this author's work. One of Dr. Albert A. Berg's first purchases was a Dickens novel in parts, and he retained a lifelong interest and affection for Dickens. Having made possible the addition of two other major Dickens collections, those of W. T. H. Howe and Owen D. Young, Dr. Berg left to New Yorkers a living memorial of Charles Dickens. Manuscript fragments of stories and novels, autograph letters, and first editions; memories of Dickens as theatrical manager, actor, and playwright; playbills of his own novels turned into plays and those plays whose leads he acted; illustrations by Dickens's contemporary illustrators, crowd a lengthy wall in the Berg Collection.

In observing the centennial celebrations the Library joins Britain in honoring its greatest novelist who, although his will instructed that no memorial be mounted in his honor, could also assert his claim to posterity in the following: "I rest my claims to the remembrance of my country upon my published works, and to the remembrance of my friends upon their experience of me in addition thereto."

Lola L. Szladits
Curator of the Berg Collection

CHARLES DICKENS
BORN FEBRUARY THE SEVENTH, 1812.
DIED JUNE THE NINTH, 1870.

"I have been very fortunate in worldly matters. Many men have worked much harder and not succeeded half so well; but I never could have done what I have done without the habits of punctuality, order and diligence; without the determination to concentrate myself on one object at a time, no matter how quickly its successor should come upon its heels, which I then formed. Heaven knows I write this in no spirit of self-laudation. The man who reviews his own life, as I do mine, in going on here, from page to page, had need to have been a good man indeed, if he would be spared the sharp consciousness of many talents neglected, many opportunities wasted, many erratic and perverted feelings constantly at war within his breast, and defeating him. I do not hold one natural gift, I dare say, that I have not abused. My meaning simply is, that whatever I have tried to do in life, I have tried with all my heart to do well; that whatever I have devoted myself to, I have devoted myself to completely; that in great aims and in small, I have always been thoroughly earnest."

(*David Copperfield*, Chapter XLII.)

George Cruikshank. Portrait sketches of Charles Dickens sketched from life, *ca.* 1837.

"It is related that Dickens and Cruikshank were members of a Club of literary men, which was known, during its brief existence, as the Hook and Eye Club, and that at one of their nightly meetings Dickens was seated in an arm-chair, conversing, when Cruikshank exclaimed, 'Sit still, Charles, while I take your portrait!' "

(Frederic G. Kitton, *Charles Dickens by pen and pencil*, London, 1890-1892.)

CHARLES DICKENS.

Entered according to Act of Congress, in the year 1867, by J. GURNEY & SON, in the Clerk's Office of the District Court of the United States, for the Southern District of New York.

P. Gurney & Son   *707 Broadway, N.Y.*

"Very different was Dickens's face in those days from that which photography made familiar to a later generation. Its look of youthfulness blended with a rare frankness of expression. The features were very good. He had a capital forehead, a firm nose with full wide nostril, eyes wonderfully beaming with intellect and running over with humour and cheerfulness, and a rather prominent mouth strongly marked with sensibility . . . The hair so scant and grizzled in later days was then of a rich brown and most luxurious abundance, and the bearded face of his last two decades had hardly a vestige of hair or whisker . . ."

(John Forster, *Forster's Life of Dickens. Abridged and revised by George Gissing*, London, 1903.)

Portrait photograph of Charles Dickens taken in 1867 during his American tour.

"To begin my life with the beginning of my life, I record that I was born (as I have been informed and believe) on a Friday, at twelve o'clock at night. It was remarked that the clock began to strike, and I began to cry simultaneously."

(*David Copperfield*, Chapter I.)

Photograph of Dickens's birthplace at Landport in Portsea.

In 1824, while Dickens's father was in the debtors' prison, the Marshalsea, a back-attic was found for Dickens at the house of an insolvent-court agent. He and his family live on in the Garlands of the *Old Curiosity Shop*.

Photograph of the house in Lant Street, London.

"I know I do not exaggerate, unconsciously and unintentionally, the scantiness of my resources or the difficulties of my life. I know that if a shilling were given me by Mr. Quinion at any time, I spent it in a dinner or a tea. I know that I worked from morning until night, with common men and boys, a shabby child. I know that I lounged about the streets, insufficiently and unsatisfactorily fed. I know that, but for the mercy of God, I might easily have been, for any care that was taken of me, a little robber or a little vagabond."

(*David Copperfield*, Chapter XI.)

"The elder Dickens furnished suggestions for the character of Mr. Micawber (as his wife did for Mrs. Nickleby). The rhetorical exuberance impressed itself upon [Dickens] later, and from this, as it expanded and developed in a thousand amusing ways, the full-length figure took its great charm. Thus it delighted Dickens to remember that it was of one of his connections his father wrote the celebrated sentence: 'And I must express my tendency to believe that his longevity is (to say the least of it) extremely problematical.' "

(John Forster, *Forster's Life of Dickens. Abridged and revised by George Gissing.*)

"Annual income twenty pounds, annual expenditure nineteen nineteen six, result happiness. Annual income twenty pounds, annual expenditure twenty pounds ought and six, result misery."

(*David Copperfield*, Chapter XII.)

Mr. Micawber. Detail from illustration by "Phiz" (Hablôt K. Browne) from the first edition of *David Copperfield*.

Letter from John Dickens, father of Charles Dickens, to his son's publishers, Chapman and Hall. London, December 19, 1837.

18 Upper Kep[pel] Street
Bloomsbury
19 Dec.ʳ 1837

Confidential

My dear Sirs

If Country people who do not know my address will trouble you with my letters, I beg you to understand I am not to blame, & I will send you my unended address in case anyone should take a similar liberty in future.

My establishment is now reduced to the lowest possible scale, and I am in hopes that with the strictest economy I shall be enabled, with the forbearance of kind friends, to work out of some annoying difficulties within the next twelve months. I have not forgot how I stand with you but in consequence of your kind offer of being willing to receive the amount at my conscience, I have deferred your claim, until more pressing demands, such as threatened my liberty, are satisfied.

I am most gratified & thankful for the great delicacy you have observed in reference to this matter, as between Charles & myself, — had it been promulgated I am sure it would have led to a breach of a most distressing nature.

I have not heard how the subscription gets on for the Volume, I trust however, that you have no reason to be dissatisfied, and that it will go off to use a contradiction in terms, in "numbers".

Pray accept my best thanks & believe me
Your ever obliged Servᵗ
John Dickens.

The volume referred to is *The Posthumous Papers of the Pickwick Club*, which had appeared in 1836-1837 in monthly numbers. 1837 also saw its first appearance in book form.

"It was Covent Garden Theatre that I chose, and there, from the back of a centre box, I saw *Julius Caesar* and the new Pantomime. To have all those noble Romans alive before me, and walking in and out for my entertainment, instead of being the stern taskmasters they had been at school, was a most novel and delightful effect. But the mingled reality and mystery of the whole show, the influence upon me of the poetry, the lights, the music, the company, the smooth stupendous changes of glittering and brilliant scenery, were so dazzling, and opened up such illimitable regions of delight, that when I came out into the rainy street, at twelve o'clock at night, I felt as if I had come from the clouds, where I had been leading a romantic life for ages, to a bawling, splashing, link-lighted, umbrella-struggling, hackney-coach-jostling, patten-clinking, muddy, miserable world."

(*David Copperfield*, Chapter XIX.)

For a short time Dickens was employed by a solicitor, afterwards, from May, 1827 to November, 1828, in the office of an attorney. If in his childhood Dickens showed early talent for singing and story-telling, at sixteen a fellow clerk promoted his taste for theatricals. They took every opportunity of going together to a "minor" theatre. The only theatres licensed to present the spoken drama were the so-called "major" theatres at Covent Garden, Drury Lane, and the Haymarket.

"He went to theatres almost every night for a long time; studied and practised himself in parts; was so much attracted by the 'At Homes' of the elder Mathews that he resolved to make his first plunge in a similar direction; and finally wrote to make offer of himself to Covent Garden. An appointment was granted him by the stage manager, but illness intervened, and Dickens wrote to say that he would resume his application next season. Success in journalism turned his thoughts elsewhere; and the stage, though it influenced his life to the end in many ways, no longer attracted him as a means of subsistence."

(John Forster, *Forster's Life of Dickens. Abridged and revised by George Gissing.*)

Letter to Amelia Austin [London, April 6? 1833].

My dear Miss Austin

Will you allow me to forward you a copy of the Prologue? A very great press of business has prevented my bestowing more than a couple of hours on the whole composition; copy and all; and I therefore trust to your usual kindness to excuse the very unladylike manner in which it is copied.

I propose (of course subject to your approval) that our first Rehearsal shall be on this day week. You know I suppose that at last we have been enabled to create a Duke.

If the space of half a sheet of paper, or the powers of a bad steel pen, — or the time of your humble Servant would admit of a description of my disappointment at not being enabled to claim the promised quadrille I should attempt it but as my feelings "may be more easily conceived than described", I shall only beg you to Believe me
                    Most truly Yours
                    Charles Dickens
I forgot the date which I
believe is

                    Saturday Morning
Fanny says "of course we see them tomorrow evening" — So say I.

Amelia Austin's brother Henry married Dickens's sister Letitia in 1837.

The "first Rehearsal" mentioned in the letter refers to *Clari; or, The Maid of Milan*, an opera in two acts by John Howard Payne, music by Henry R. Bishop, first performed in 1823. It is now forgotten except for one immortal song, "Home Sweet Home." The playbill for *Clari* (see p. 8) is the earliest known on which Dickens's name appears both as stage manager and as actor. The company was made up of his friends and relations.

"I feel as if it were not for me to record, even though this manuscript is intended for no eyes but mine, how hard I worked at that tremendous shorthand, and all improvement appertaining to it . . . I will only add to what I have already written of my perseverance at this time of my life, and of a patient and continuous energy which then began to be matured within me, and which I know to be the strong part of my character, if it have any strength at all, that there, on looking back, I find the source of my success."

(*David Copperfield*, Chapter XLII.)

Private Theatricals.

STAGE MANAGER, MR. CHARLES DICKENS.

ON SATURDAY EVENING, APRIL 27, 1833,

At Seven o'clock precisely. The performances will commence with

AN INTRODUCTORY PROLOGUE;

THE PRINCIPAL CHARACTERS BY

MR. EDWARD BARROW; MR. MILTON; MR. CHARLES DICKENS; MISS AUSTIN; AND MISS DICKENS.

IMMEDIATELY AFTER WHICH WILL BE PRESENTED THE OPERA OF

CLARI.

The Duke Vivaldi	MR. BRAMWELL,
Rolamo, a Farmer, (Father to Clari)	MR. C. DICKENS,
Jocoso, (Valet to the Duke)	MR. H. AUSTIN,
Nicolo	MR. MILTON,
Geronio	MR. E. BARROW,
Nimpedo	MR. R. AUSTIN,
Pages to the Duke	MASTERS F. DICKENS & A. DICKENS.
Clari	MISS DICKENS,
Fidalma (her Mother)	MISS L. DICKENS,
Vespina	MISS AUSTIN,
Ninetta	MISS OPPENHEIM.

CHARACTERS IN THE EPISODE.

The Nobleman	MR. HENRY KOLLE,
Pelgrino, a Farmer	MR. JOHN DICKENS,
Wife of Pelgrino	MISS URQUHART,
Leoda	MISS OPPENHEIM.

AFTER WHICH THE FAVOURITE INTERLUDE OF

The Married Bachelor.

Sir Charles Courtall	MR. C. DICKENS,
Sharp	MR. JOHN URQUHART,
Lady Courtall	MISS L. DICKENS,
Grace	MISS DICKENS.

TO CONCLUDE WITH THE FARCE OF

Amateurs & Actors.

David Dulcet, Esq. (a Musical Dramatic Amateur, who employs Mr. O. P. Bustle, and attached to Theatricals and Miss Mary Hardacre)	MR. H. AUSTIN,
Mr. O. P. Bustle, (a Provincial Manager, but engaged to superintend some Private Theatricals)	MR. BRAMWELL,
Wing, (a poor Country Actor)	MR. C. DICKENS,
Berry, (an Actor for the heavy Business)	MR. BOSTON,
Elderberry, (a retired Manufacturer, simple in wit and manners, and utterly unacquainted with Theatricals)	MR. J. DICKENS,
Timkins, (Elderberry's Factotum)	MR. R. AUSTIN,
Geoffry Muffincap, (an elderly Charity Boy, let out as a Servant at Bustle's Lodging)	MR. E. BARROW,
Miss Mary Hardacre, (a fugitive Ward of Elderberry's	MISS DICKENS,
Mrs. Mary Goneril, (a Strolling Tragedy Actress, and a serious evil to her Husband)	MISS OPPENHEIM

The Scenery by Messrs. H. Austin, Milton, H. Kolle, and Assistants.———The Band which will be numerous and complete, under the direction of Mr. E. Barrow.

J. & G. Nichols, Printers, Earl's Court, Cranbourn Street, Soho.

Private Theatricals, April 27, 1833.

At nineteen he became a Parliamentary reporter. Among the eighty or ninety reporters he occupied the very highest rank, not merely for accuracy in reporting, but for marvelous quickness in transcript. While still on the *Mirror of Parliament* he tried unsuccessfully for a post on the *Morning Chronicle*. He did, however, as he later said, drop "with fear and trembling into a dark letter-box in a dark office up a dark court in Fleet Street," a sketch which first appeared in the *Monthly Magazine* and then in *Sketches by Boz*. His new-found character is reflected also in further theatrical pieces he composed.

The newly built St. James's Theatre prompted Dickens to write a small farce in aid of the enterprise (*The Strange Gentleman*, London, Chapman and Hall, 1837). This "comic burletta" was an adaptation of "The Great Winglebury Duel" in *Sketches by Boz* [First Series]. The first performance also opened the season of 1836 and the play was performed for sixty nights. Its popularity was mainly due to the ability of J. P. Harley, actor and stage manager, for whom the farce was written.

Although the first edition is excessively rare, the Berg Collection possesses three copies, one of which has markings showing that it has been used as a prompt copy in the stage production.

Hablôt K. Browne ("Phiz"). "The Strange Gentleman. Act 1. Scene 1." Original pencil drawing for the frontispiece. Inserted in a copy of the rare first edition.

John Leech, an aspiring young illustrator five years Dickens's junior, hoped amongst other applicants that he would be selected as the artist for *The Pickwick Papers* when Robert Seymour committed suicide. He was not. This drawing, however, pleased Dickens who wrote: "I think he has not got the face well, or the hat. The general character is very good."

John Leech. "J. P. Harley in the role of The strange gentleman." Original pencil and water color drawing. Inserted in a copy of the 1837 facsimile reprint published by Chapman and Hall.

Letter to Richard Bentley [August 27? 1836].

Mrs. Denman's. Petersham near Richmond
Saturday Evening

My Dear Sir.

    I don't know whether you have seen any of the "rumours" which have appeared in the papers, about my forthcoming opera at Braham's. It has excited some curiosity, inasmuch as it will be the first time for many years, that a "drama" has been united to music, or poetry to songs: and a great many competent judges who have heard it, consider it to possess both, in a high degree.

    It has occurred to me recently, that if it should make a very great hit, and were published during the run, it would be very likely to have a considerable sale. "Boz's" first play — an old English story, and an attempt to revive the rustic opera — would, I think be purchased, if it were published at any reasonable price. Supposing it should be as successful as I, and everyone else anticipate, should you feel disposed to make any agreement with me, for publishing it? I merely ask the question in order that I may know how to act. You can either see the Manuscript now, or be present at the first representation; or both. I may add that the Music (of which I have half the copyright) is purchased for a large sum, and the whole affair is expected to go off with great eclat. It will be produced about the middle of October.

    If you will consider the matter, and favor me with your answer, here, I shall be much obliged to you: — I can call, and talk it over, if you think it worth while.

I am
Dear Sir
Very faithfully Yours
Charles Dickens

PS. Of course I do not like to say — of my own production that it is a good one; and therefore before we made any distinct agreement, I should like you to see it played, or to read it. If it were published at all, it would be most desirable to have it out, immediately after it had "taken". Mr. Hogarth is a good authority in these cases, and he prognosticates wonders.

Dickens wrote the libretto for the music of his friend John Hullah. The first performance took place at the St. James's Theatre on December 6, 1836. Dickens rejected his work years later and begged that it might be allowed to "sink into its native obscurity."

    About a year before his death Dickens was asked by Frederick Locker whether he owned a copy of *The Village Coquettes*. The reply was: "No; and if I knew it was in my house, and if I could not get rid of it in any other way, I would burn the wing of the house where it was!"

If there was a contemporaneous publication of *Is She His Wife?* in 1837, it is supposedly extinct. No copies of it are recorded. The "bibliographer's first edition" is considered to be the 1877 reprint by James R. Osgood of Boston.

St. James's Theatre Playbill for *Is She His Wife?* April 6, 1837. *The Strange Gentleman* and *The Village Coquettes* also listed.

Letter to John Pritt Harley [London, January 21? 1837].

Furnivals Inn.
Saturday Evening.

My Dear Sir.

Between the anxieties of my private affairs, and the distractions of my public engagements, I have not yet got over Pickwick and the Miscellany and consequently can admit no "other lodger" into my brain at this moment. I have by me a little piece in one act called "Cross Purposes", which I wrote long before I was Boz. It would admit of the introduction of any Music; and if you think there is anything in it, it is at your service.

I had intended to send the MS to you to-night, but if you are likely to be at home and disengaged at any reasonable hour tomorrow, I will call with it in my pocket, and discuss affairs in general.

You can send me a verbal answer by my brother. Of course the Lodger will be forthcoming.

Faithfully Yours my dear Sir,
Charles Dickens

"Cross Purposes" became *Is She His Wife? or Something Singular*, a comic burletta in one act; first performed at St. James's, March 6, 1837, with J. P. Harley in the chief role.

Letter to John Pritt Harley [London, April 7, 1837].

48 Doughty Street
Friday Morning

My Dear Sir

Have the goodness in the bills of the Village Coquettes to omit all mention of our respectable friend "Boz". After the choppings and changings which this most unfortunate of all unfortunate pieces has undergone, I am not anxious to remind the Public that I am the perpetrator.

Faithfully Yours
Charles Dickens

The name "Boz" was first omitted from the playbills of the 8th April, having appeared in playbills for the 6th and 7th.

THE

Theatrical Observer;
AND
Daily Bills of the Play.

"Nothing extenuate, nor set down aught in malice."—*Othello.*

No. 4682.   Monday, Dec. 19, 1836.   Price 1d.

" The Play's the thing"—Ask for *Thomas's Observer.*

COVENT GARDEN THEATRE.

Romeo and Juliet and *Charles the Twelfth* were performed here on Saturday night to a crowded audience. Charles Kemble personated *Mercutio,* and the Merry Monarch, each for the last time. Miss Vincent made an interesting *Mary Copp.*

DRURY LANE THEATRE.

THERE was a very elegant audience here on Saturday night, to witness the representation of *The Wrecker's Daughter,* and the new Grand Ballet. A new petite Comedy. in two acts, is in rehearsal, as is Barnett's new Opera of *Fair Rosamond,* the score of which arrived from Paris last week. There is a talk of Miss De Lacy, making her *debut* at this Theatre as a singer ; she has played *Cinderella,* at Leeds, with great success ; she is a daughter and pupil of Rophino Lacy.

NEW ENGLISH OPERA HOUSE.

As we anticipated, Mr. Mitchell's experiment of establishing an Opera Buffa is likely to prove decidedly successful ; each night the audience has become more numerous, and on Saturday, when Donizetti's semi seria Opera of *Il Furioso* was performed, the house was crowded in every part, and an additional row of stalls had been made for the accommodation of the public. The Opera which has had a great run at LaScala at Milan, contains some charming music, especially in the second act, but as the airs for the tenore were thought rather weak, Balfe composed two for Catone, one of which, with a horn obligato, (delightfully played by Puzzi,) is a delicious *morceau.* There were three *debuts,* Ronconi, a barytone, who sang with exquisite taste and feeling, Ruggiero, a basso, who is an excellent comic actor, and *la prima donna,* Signora Luini, who came here with a great reputation ; which reputation, we, however, are bound to say, she did not sustain. It might be that diffidence impeded her powers, and this we are rather inclined to think, as in the second act, especially in the finale, she improved vastly. Miss Glossop, from the St. James's Theatre, was *la seconda donna,* and a far better one than we are accustomed to have in such *roles* ; she has a very good voice, and is an excellent musician.

THE ST. JAMES'S THEATRE,

On Saturday night *The Village Coquettes,* the attraction of which increases rather than diminishes, was repeated to a fashionable and numerous audience, and went off with the greatest éclat. The music of this Opera is purely English, and its touching and, beautiful melodies are calculated to please not only the scientific, but also the unlearned in musical matters. Braham, was in fine voice, and sang his portion of the music delightfully ;

E. & J. THOMAS, Printers, 6, Exeter Street, Strand.

The Theatrical Observer; and Daily Bills of the Play, [London]
No. 4682, December 19, 1836, commenting on
The Village Coquettes.

"In humble imitation of a prudent course, universally adopted by aeronauts, the Author of these volumes throws them up as his pilot balloon, trusting it may catch some favourable current, and devoutly and earnestly hoping it may *go off well* — a sentiment in which his Publisher cordially concurs."

(*Sketches by "Boz,"* First Series, Preface.)

Encouraged by the success of the first "Sketch" in the *Monthly Magazine* in December 1833 Dickens contributed eight more, the last of which was published in February 1835. "They bore no signature until August 1834, when he adopted the pseudonym of 'Boz' — a very familiar household word to him, being the nickname of his youngest brother Augustus, whom he had dubbed Moses, in honour of the Vicar of Wakefield — this, being facetiously pronounced through the nose, became Boses, and when shortened, became Boz."

(Frederic G. Kitton, *Charles Dickens; his life, writings, and personality*, London, 1902.)

"Who the *dickens* 'Boz' could be
   Puzzled many a learned elf,
Till time unveiled the mystery,
   And 'Boz' appeared as Dickens' self."

(*Bentley's Miscellany*, March, 1837.)

The name "Boz" remained coupled with "inimitable" until "Boz" disappeared and throughout his career left Dickens known as "The Inimitable."

Early in 1835, one of the editors of the *Morning Chronicle*, George Hogarth, Dickens's future father-in-law, made arrangements for an evening edition of that paper. The *Evening Chronicle*, launched on January 31, 1835, contained until the following August further "Sketches" by "Boz."

Dickens wisely retained the copyright. He disposed of it to John Macrone, who in 1836 published a selection of the published articles supplemented by eight new ones. The renowned artist, George Cruikshank, supplied the etchings. In 1837 there appeared a Second Series, following which Chapman and Hall issued the first Complete Edition, containing both series, in monthly parts from 1837 to 1839.

The engraved title page of the Second Series and that of the Complete Edition reflect the artist's rendering of the author's metaphor in the "Preface." Two figures, closely resembling Charles Dickens and George Cruikshank, wave from the car of the rising balloon.

Draft of a letter from George Cruikshank to John Macrone [London, 1836].

My Dr Sir

The arrangement with Mr. Dickens was that I was to have the choise [sic] of a quantity of "Sketches" to select subjects from — & not to be compeled [sic] to illustrate those only which might be sent as a matter of course — & in order that the work might be got out in good time I was to have been supplied with the copy some months back. Now I have only rec.^d those said two Sketches — & the moment I got them — they were read & my memoranda made — & duly deposited under a cover marke[d] Illuts. [sic] by Boz Vol. 2 — since which I have been in daily expectation of seeing others — & indeed expecting the whole & have felt puzzled & surprised at their non appearance — indeed I have been waiting for them untill [sic] I could wait no longer & with submission to you I do not . . .

Letter to George Cruikshank [London, January 7? 1836].

Furnivals Inn
Thursday Morning

My Dear Sir.
As I have mentioned your name in the accompanying little preface to my book, I think it better to inclose it for your perusal, although I hope you will find nothing in it to object to. It will be sent to the printer's in the course of tomorrow, and you will perhaps have the kindness to return it to my messenger tomorrow morning — he will call for that purpose.
Pray make my compliments to Mrs Cruikshank and Believe me
Dear Sir
Very Sincerely Yours
Charles Dickens

Dickens refers to the Preface of *Sketches by "Boz"*.

Letter to George Thomson, Mrs. Dickens's maternal grandfather. February 27, 1836.

15 Furnivals Inn. London.
February 27th 1836.

My Dear Sir

I feel a degree of pleasure I cannot describe, in begging your acceptance, of the accompanying Volumes; — not because it gratifies an Author's vanity, but because it affords me an opportunity of paying a very slight tribute of remembrance and respect, to such near Relatives of my dear Catherine as yourself, and Mrs. Thomson.

As I do not despair of seeing you both at Catherine's table, before any very long time has elapsed (indeed, we think you ought to indulge us, by making a journey to London on purpose) I will only add, that I most sincerely and earnestly hope it may afford you half the pleasure to receive my little productions, which I promise myself, from forwarding them to you — I trust for many, many, years to come.

Begging my best remembrances to Mrs. Thomson, and everybody I ought to know, but most unfortunately do not —

I am
My Dear Sir
Most Sincerely Yours
Charles Dickens

The copy of *Sketches by "Boz"* presented to George Thomson is now in the Berg Collection.

"I have come out in another way. I have taken with fear and trembling to authorship. I wrote a little something, in secret, and sent it to a magazine, and it was published in the magazine. Since then I have taken heart to write a good many trifling pieces. Now, I am regularly paid for them. Altogether, I am well-off; when I tell my income on the fingers of my left hand, I pass the third finger and take in the fourth to the middle joint."

(*David Copperfield*, Chapter XLIII.)

Sketches by Boz. No. 1 [November 1837]-No. 20 [June, 1839], London, Chapman and Hall. The illustration is of No. 8.

Public Dinners.

Sketches by Boz, No. 8, contained George Cruikshank's celebrated etching, "Public Dinners," where he again portrayed Dickens and himself.

George Cruikshank. "Scotland Yard." Original pen and
ink and water color drawing. Inserted in a copy of
Sketches by Boz. New Edition. Complete.
London, 1839.

"Bright and pleasant was the sky, balmy the air, and beautiful the appearance of every object around, as Mr. Pickwick leaned over the balustrades of Rochester Bridge, contemplating nature, and waiting for breakfast. The scene was indeed one which might well have charmed a far less reflective mind than that to which it was presented."

(*The Posthumous Papers of the Pickwick Club*, Chapter V.)

"It is the fate of most men who mingle with the world, and attain even the prime of life, to make many real friends, and lose them in the course of nature. It is the fate of all authors or chroniclers to create imaginary friends, and lose them in the course of art. Nor is this the full extent of their misfortunes; for they are required to furnish an account of them besides."

(*The Posthumous Papers of the Pickwick Club*, Chapter LVI.)

"When you have parted with a man at two o'clock in the morning on terms of the utmost good fellowship, and he meets you again at half-past nine and greets you as a serpent, it is not unreasonable to conclude that something of an unpleasant nature has occurred meanwhile."

(*The Posthumous Papers of the Pickwick Club*, Chapter XVII.)

"I laboured hard at my book, without allowing it to interfere with the punctual discharge of my newspaper duties, and it came out and was very successful. I was not stunned by the praise which sounded in my ears, notwithstanding that I was keenly alive to it, and thought better of my own performance, I have little doubt, than anybody else did. It has always been in my observation of human nature that a man who has any good reason to believe in himself never flourishes himself before the faces of other people in order that they may believe in him. For this reason, I retained my modesty in very self-respect, and the more praise I got, the more I tried to deserve."

(*David Copperfield*, Chapter XLVIII.)

". . . I do not enter on the aspirations, the delights, anxieties, and triumphs of my art. That I truly devoted myself to it with my strongest earnestness, and bestowed upon it every energy of my soul, I have already said. If the books I have written be of any worth, they will supply the rest. I shall otherwise have written to poor purpose, and the rest will be of interest to no one."

(*David Copperfield*, Chapter LXI.)

"During these same weeks, despite all these preoccupations and his work on *Pickwick*, Dickens made the time to indite an angry pamphlet which is significant of his entire viewpoint at this period. Toward the end of April he had listened indignantly to the reintroduction in Parliament of a bill offered by Sir Andrew Agnew that would have prohibited not merely all work but all recreation on Sunday... By working at top speed, he got it in print by June, signed with the pseudonym "Timothy Sparks.""

(Edgar Johnson, *Charles Dickens*, New York, 1952.)

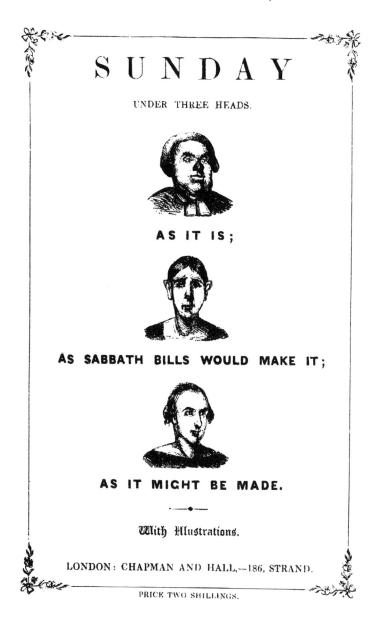

Sunday Under Three Heads. As It Is; As Sabbath Bills Would Make It; As It Might Be Made. By Timothy Sparks. London, Chapman and Hall, [1836].

Letter to Chapman and Hall [London, February 18, 1836].

Furnivals Inn.
Thursday Evening

Dr Sirs.

Pickwick is at length begun in all his might and glory. The first chapter, will be ready to-morrow.

I want to publish the Strange Gentleman. If you have no objection to doing it, I should be happy to let you have the refusal of it. I need not say that nobody else, has seen or heard of it.

Believe me (in Pickwickian haste)
Faithfully yours
Charles Dickens

William Hall, the partner of Edward Chapman, visited "Boz" in person early in 1836, to ask him whether he would write the text to Robert Seymour's plates portraying sporting characters. Although a great walker himself, Dickens was not a sportsman and the idea did not appeal to him. The *Times*, when announcing the new project on March 26, 1836, gave the outline: "...a faithful record of the Perambulations, Perils, Travels, Adventures, and Sporting Transactions of the Corresponding Members of the Pickwick Club." The name Pickwick was accidentally seen by Dickens on the door of a Bath coach owned by Moses Pickwick. Sam Weller was suggested by a character in a play by Beazeley. A popular low comedian, Samuel Vale, assumed the part and entertained his audience by quaint sayings and out-of-the-way comparisons.

Letter to Richard Bentley [London, January 7, 1837].

Furnivals Inn
Saturday Morning

My Dear Sir.

After a day and night of watching and anxiety, I was yesterday made — not a Member of the Garrick Club; but a father. Need I, under such circumstances, beg you to postpone our appointment from 12 oClock to day, until ½ past 3 in order that I may have time for a little rest? —

Believe me
Dear Sir
Faithfully Yours
Charles Dickens

The first of Dickens's ten children, Charles Culliford Boz Dickens, was born on January 6, 1837.

Letter to Richard Bentley [London, May 8, 1837].

48 Doughty Street
Monday Morning

My Dear Sir.

I am most sorry to inform you that Mrs. Dickens' sister whom you saw here, after accompanying us to the Theatre on Saturday Evening in the best health and spirits, was taken suddenly ill, and died in my arms yesterday afternoon — since which time her mother has been also lying here in a state of insensibility. She was our constant friend and companion, and the loss independent of its fearful suddenness, is severely felt by us. I have given the Printer matter to go on with, and tomorrow or at furthest next day, will send him more. I must entreat you to spare me in the meanwhile.

Dear Sir
Faithfully Yours
Charles Dickens

Shortly after the wedding of April 2, 1836, in which Charles Dickens married Catherine (Kate) Hogarth, the bride's young sister of sixteen, Mary Hogarth, moved in with the young couple at Doughty Street. When she died on May 7, 1837, Dickens sank into an agony of grief. Until the day he died, he wore on his own finger a ring that he had slipped from her lifeless one. He himself composed the inscription for Mary's tombstone and for many years he continued to dream of her. There was no number of *Pickwick* for the end of May and work begun on *Oliver Twist* was delayed.

Letter to William Harrison Ainsworth [London, May 17, 1837].

Collins's Farm. North End. Hampstead
Wednesday Evening

My Dear Ainsworth.

I have been so much unnerved and hurt by the loss of the dear girl whom I loved, after my wife, more deeply and fervently than anyone on earth, that I have been compelled for once to give up all idea of my monthly work, and to try a fortnight's rest and quiet. We have hired a very small cottage here, and have repaired hither for a little change of air and scene.

I believe there is some cross road which leads out very near your house. I wish you would show me the way by coming here. You cannot think how glad I should be to see you just now. I have given you the address above, and must leave the rest to you.

With compliments to the Ladies
Believe me
Most Faithfully Yours
Charles Dickens

spoken in a very loud tone, but she understood
him at once, and drank off a full glass
of wine to his long life and happiness; after
which, the worthy old soul launched
forth into a minute and particular
account of her own wedding, with a
dissertation on high-heeled shoes *the fashion of wearing* ~~and~~
~~and~~ some particulars concerning the
life and adventures of the beautiful Lady
Tollinglower *deceased*, at all of which the old
Lady ~~~~ herself laughed very heartily
indeed, and so did the young ladies too,
for they were wondering among themselves
what on earth Grandma was talking
about. When they laughed, the old
lady laughed ten times more heartily, and
said that they always had been considered
capital stories, which caused them all
to laugh again, and ~~their~~ put the old lady
into the very best of humours. ✝(see back)

"Mr Miller" said Mr Pickwick to
his old acquaintance, the hard-headed gentleman "a glass of wine?"
"With great satisfaction Mr Pickwick"
replied the hard-headed gentleman solemnly.
"You'll take me in?" said the
benevolent old clergyman.

The story became popular only when Sam Weller was introduced in Chapter 10, the fourth number of the monthly parts. With *Pickwick* Dickens started his practice of giving a final "double number," — two parts bound in one.

No. I.]

[HE

POSTHUMOUS PAPERS

OF THE

PICKWICK CLUB

CONTAINING A FAITHFUL RECORD OF THE

PERAMBULATIONS, PERILS, TRAVELS, ADVENTURES

AND

Sporting Transactions

OF THE CORRESPONDING MEMBERS.

EDITED BY "BOZ."

WITH FOUR ILLUSTRATIONS.
BY SEYMOUR

LONDON: CHAPMAN & HALL, 186, STRAND.

MDCCCXXXVI

[PRICE 1s.

The Posthumous Papers of the Pickwick Club. No. 1 [April, 1836]-
No. 19-20 [November, 1837]. London, Chapman and Hall.
No. 1 is illustrated here.

Letter to Mrs. Henry Stephens Belcombe, London, February 8, 1838.

Mr. Charles Dickens presents his best compliments to Mrs. Henry Belcombe, and begs her acceptance of one of a few copies of the Pickwick Papers, which the zeal of his publishers has put into a much smarter dress than his own modesty might have suggested as an appropriate costume. He ventures to forward it to Mrs. Belcombe as a slight acknowledgment of the great kindness and attention he received from her family in his recent visit to York, and of the great pleasure he derived from their society.

48 Doughty Street London
February 8th 1838.

This is the first complete edition in book form. The copy presented to Mrs. Belcombe is inscribed: "With sincerest regards," and was bound in blue Levant morocco, with gilt edges, by Rivière.

The Posthumous Papers of the Pickwick Club. London, Chapman and Hall, 1837.

Letter to Samuel Lover [London, November 16, 1837].

48 Doughty Street
Thursday Morning

My dear Lover.

There is a semi-business semi-pleasure kind of dinner in honor of the completion of Pickwick, to come off on Saturday at Degex's the Prince of Wales Leicester Place Leicester Square at 5 o'Clock for half past 5 precisely. If you will make one of my guests you will gratify me exceedingly. Talfourd and Macready and one or two more will be there to counterbalance the publishers and printers, so I hope I can promise you a tolerably pleasant evening.

I would have given you longer notice, but having to consider the engagements of different members of the party, I have only just been able to "name the day".

Write me a line off-hand like a decent Irishman (if there be such a thing) and say you'll come.

Believe me Ever
Faithfully Yours
Charles Dickens

"The dinner and the wines, Ainsworth said, were both capital. And Jerdan recalled that at the table 'the pleasant and uncommon fact was stated . . . that there never had been a line of written agreement, but that the author, printer, artist, and publisher had all proceeded on simple verbal assurances, and that there never had arisen a word to interrupt the complete satisfaction of everyone.' . . . In the course of the evening Dickens received from his publishers a set of silver 'Apostle' spoons with characters from *Pickwick*. . . . And, only eight months after the modest *Pickwick* dinner, he received what almost amounted to official recognition as one of England's celebrities."

(Edgar Johnson, *Charles Dickens*.)

Letter to Thomas Noon Talfourd [London, October 4, 1837].

Doughty Street
Wednesday Night

My dear Talfourd.

I write a line before going to bed, just to say that no preparation for my trip Peak-wise or otherwise will prevent my having the great pleasure of a trip with you either on Friday or Saturday if your engagements will permit — and that I shall look anxiously for the note in which you fix your own time.

Murray, supposing I presume that any notice in the Quarterly must drive so young a man as myself nearly distracted with delight, sent me the Quarterly yesterday. I think Hayward has <u>rather</u> *visited upon me his recollection of my declining his intimate acquaintance, but as the Notice contains a great deal that I know to be true, and much more which may be, but of which I am no impartial judge, I find little fault with it. I hope I may truly say that no writer ever had less vanity than I have; and that my only anxiety to stand well with the world in that capacity, originates in authorship being unhappily my trade, as it is happily my pleasure.*

I am sorry you blush to think of "that other matter" — even in modesty. I wish I had any better means of assuring you how honestly and sincerely I am your most affectionate and attached friend.

Ever Faithfully Yours
Charles Dickens

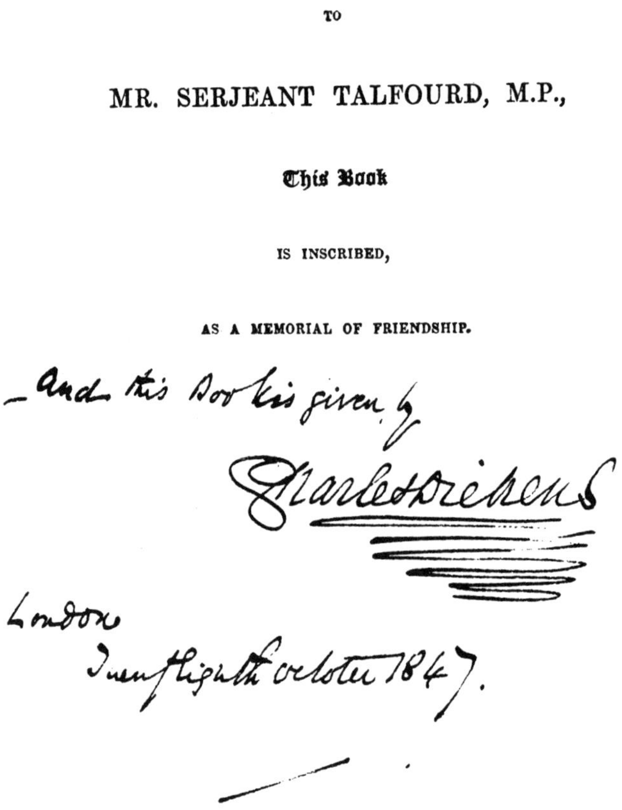

TO

MR. SERJEANT TALFOURD, M.P.,

𝕿𝖍𝖎𝖘 𝕭𝖔𝖔𝖐

IS INSCRIBED,

AS A MEMORIAL OF FRIENDSHIP.

And this Book is given by

Charles Dickens

London
Twenty Eighth October 1847.

Dedication page of *The Posthumous Papers of the Pickwick Club*, London, Chapman and Hall, 1847.

"That other matter" mentioned in the letter to Thomas Noon Talfourd was Dickens's request to allow him to dedicate the book to him. This copy of a late edition is therefore a dedication copy of sorts. On the dedication page the author inscribed it for his friend.

Letter to the Editor of the *Durham Advertiser*, Darlington [February 3, 1838].

Darlington
Saturday Morning

Sir.

　Waiting in this place for a York coach this morning, I chanced in the course of the few minutes I stayed here, to take up your paper of January the 26th in which I saw a brief Auto-biography of myself by Dr. Mackenzie. Dr. Mackenzie whoever he may be, knows as much of me as of the meaning of the word autobiography, in proof of which may I beg you to state on my authority that when I commenced the Pickwick papers I was <u>not</u> living on five guineas a week as a Reporter on the Morning Chronicle — that Messrs. Chapman and Hall were never persuaded with some difficulty to become the Pickwick publishers but on the contrary first became known to me by waiting on me to propose the work — that no such pecuniary arrangement as the paragraph describes ever existed between us — that by the Pickwick Papers alone I have <u>not</u> netted between £2000 and £3000 — that the Sketch called Watkins Tottle never appeared in The Morning Chronicle — that I am <u>not</u> now in the receipt of £3000 a year, and that Mr. Bentley does <u>not</u> give me £1000 a year for editing the Miscellany and twenty guineas a sheet for what I write in it.

　I have the honor to be Sir
　　Your most obed^t Servant
　　Charles Dickens

Robert Seymour. "There was a fine gentle wind, and Mr. Pick-wick's hat rolled sportively be-fore it." Original pen and ink sketch to illustrate Chapter IV, Number II.

Mr Seymour died when only the first twenty-four pages printed pages of the Pickwick Papers were published; I think, before the next four pages were completely written; I am sure, before one subsequent line of the book was invented.

In the Preface to the cheap Edition of the Pickwick Papers, published in October 1847, I thus described the origin of that work.

"I was a young man of three-and-twenty, when the present publishers, attracted by some pieces I was as that time writing in the Morning Chronicle newspaper (of which one series had lately been collected and published in two volumes, illustrated by my esteemed friend MR. GEORGE CRUIKSHANK), waited upon me to propose a something that should be published in shilling numbers—then only known to me, or I believe, to anybody else, by a dim recollection of certain interminable novels in that form, which used, some five-and-twenty years ago, to be carried about the country by pedlars, and over some of which I remember to have shed innumerable tears, before I served my apprenticeship to Life.

"The idea propounded to me was that the monthly something should be a vehicle for certain plates to be executed by MR. SEYMOUR, and there was a notion, either on the part of that admirable humourous artist, or of my visitor (I forget which), that a "NIMROD Club," the members of which were to go out shooting, fishing, and so forth, and getting themselves into difficulties through their want of dexterity, would be the best means of introducing these. I objected, on consideration, that although born and partly bred in the country I was no great sportsman, except in regard of all kinds of locomotion; that the idea was not novel, and had been already much used; that it would be infinitely better for the plates to arise naturally out of the

"A History of 'Pickwick'," March 28, 1866. Manuscript draft.

Robert Seymour, the artist who so unhappily killed himself during the production of *Pickwick*, had originally suggested the subject of a Cockney sporting club. Mrs. Seymour and later her son launched attacks on Dickens and claimed that the initial success of *Pickwick* was due to Seymour. In the *Athenaeum*, March 31, 1866, Dickens gave an account of the origin of *Pickwick*.

Hablôt K. Browne ("Phiz"). Illustration for *Pickwick*, Chapter XLVI,
Number XVII, portraying Mr. and Mrs. Winkle and Mr. Pickwick.
Original pencil and wash sketch, with Dickens's comments
to the artist.

The third number of *Pickwick* announced that Robert William Buss was to become the illustrator.
However, only two of his etchings were accepted and published in that number. From among the
eager applicants, who also included John Leech and W. M. Thackeray, a young man barely twenty-one
was chosen. Hablôt K. Browne first signed himself "Nemo," but went on to explain: "I think I signed
myself as 'Nemo' to my first etchings (those of No. 4) before adopting 'Phiz' as my *sobriquet*, to har-
monize — I suppose — better with Dickens's 'Boz.' " The collaboration continued for twenty-three
years and came to an end with *A Tale of Two Cities*, 1859. As designer of the plates for ten of four-
teen principal novels by the "Inimitable Boz," his illustrator "Phiz" rightly takes his place with him
as a creator of the characters.

SCENERY.---ACT I.

INN YARD and BLACKSMITH'S SHOP!

In the VILLAGE of LONJUMEAU.

ACT II.

The BOUDOIR of Madame DE LATOUR!

Opening on a Garden.

ACT III.

THE NUPTIAL CHAMBER !

After which, an original Comic Burletta, in One Act, Written by BOZ, called

IS SHE HIS WIFE ?

Or, SOMETHING SINGULAR !

Alfred Lovetown, Esq. Mr FORESTER,   Mr Peter Limbury, Mr GARDNER,

Felix Tapkins, Esq. (*formerly of the India House Leadenhall Street,* and now of Rustic Lodge near Reading,) Mr HARLEY,

Mrs. Lovetown, Miss ALLISON,   Mrs Peter Limbury, Madame SALA.

Mr HARLEY

Will in the Character of

MR. PICKWICK

Make his First Visit

TO THE ST. JAMES'S THEATRE,

And relate, to a Scotch Air, his

EXPERIENCES

OF

"A White Bait Dinner at Blackwall."

EDITED EXPRESSLY FOR HIM BY HIS BIOGRAPHER

"BOZ!"

The whole to conclude with, (by Particular Desire) for the **58th & Last Night this Season**

THE STRANGE Gentleman.

Mr. Owen Overton (*Mayor of a Small Town on the Road to Gretna, & useful at the St. James's Arms*) Mr HOLLINGSWORTH

John Johnson   (*Detained at the St. James's Arms*)   Mr. SIDNEY,

The Strange Gentleman...............(*Just Arrived at the St. James's Arms*)................Mr. HARLEY,

Charles Tomkins.........(*Incognito at the St. James's Arms*).............Mr. FORESTER.

Tom Sparks.. ....(*a One Eyed "Boots," at the St. James's Arms*) ....Mr. GARDNER.

John......⎱   ⎰....Mr. WILLIAMSON,

Tom....⎰ *Waiters at the St. James's Arms* ⎱....Mr. MAY,

Will....⎰   ⎱....Mr. COULSON,

Julia Dobbs   (*Looking for a Husband at the St. James's Arms*)   Madame SALA,

Fanny Wilson.........(*With an Appointment at the St. James's Arms*)...........Miss SMITH,

Mary Wilson.............(*her Sister awkwardly situated at the St. James's Arms*)................Miss JULIA SMITH

Mrs. Noakes.............(*the Landlady at the St. James's Arms*) ....Mrs PENSON,

Chambermaid, (*at the St. James's Arms*) Miss STUART.

Duet—"I know a Bank,".... ......Miss SMITH and Miss JULIA SMITH.

TICKETS, BOXES, and PRIVATE BOXES, may be obtained of Mr HARLEY, 14, Upper Gower Street, Bedford Square; and of Mr W. WARNE, at the Box-Office, at the Theatre, from Eleven until Six o'Clock daily.

Boxes 5s.--Second Price 3s.   Pit 3s.--Second Price 2s.
Gallery 1s, 6d.--Second Price 1s.

St. James's Theatre Playbill for *Mr. Pickwick*, March 13, 1837.

"When my thoughts go back now to that slow agony of my youth, I wonder how much of the histories I invented for such people hangs like a mist of fancy over well-remembered facts! When I tread the old ground, I do not wonder that I seem to see and pity, going on before me, an innocent romantic boy, making his imaginative world out of such strange experiences and sordid things."

(*David Copperfield*, Chapter XI.)

"Having some foundation for believing, by this time, that nature and accident had made me an author, I pursued my vocation with confidence. Without such assurance I should certainly have left it alone, and bestowed my energy on some other endeavour. I should have tried to find out what nature and accident really had made me, and be that, and nothing else."

(*David Copperfield*, Chapter XLVIII.)

Letter to Richard Bentley, [London] November 2 [1836].

> *Furnivals Inn*
> *Wednesday Evening*
> *Novr 2nd*

My dear Sir.

I have well weighed the subject on which we conversed this morning; and feeling perfectly satisfied that it will not interfere with Pickwick, shall be happy to undertake the editorship of the new Magazine, on the following conditions being settled between us.

I should like in my agreement to have my duties specifically set forth, together with the emoluments you propose, and a stipulation relative to the quantity of matter I am to furnish monthly, which I understand is never to exceed a sheet. As I should immediately throw up my connection with the Chronicle in the event of my closing with you, I make it a sine qua non that my engagement is for a year certain. I have little doubt that it would last for many years, but as I must resign a certain income elsewhere, this condition is indispensable.

The terms I leave to you to propose. I need not enlarge on the rapidly increasing value of my time and writings to myself, or on the assistance "Boz's" name just now, would prove to the circulation, because I am persuaded that no one is better able to form a correct estimate on both points, than you are.

I thought it might facilitate our dispatch of business on Friday, if I stated these points at once. Within four and twenty hours after you make me a definite proposal, I will return a final answer. Of course I understand that until we agree to make it public, the project remains a secret.

> *I am*
> *Dear Sir*
> *Very faithfully Yours*
> *Charles Dickens*

"What an amazing place London was to me when I saw it in the distance, and how I believed all the adventures of all my favourite heroes to be constantly enacting and re-enacting there, and how I vaguely made it out in my own mind to be fuller of wonders and wickedness than all the cities of the earth, I need not stop here to relate."

(*David Copperfield*, Chapter V.)

"A dirtier or more wretched place [Oliver] had never seen. The street was very narrow and muddy, and the air was impregnated with filthy odours. There were a good many small shops; but the only stock in trade appeared to be heaps of children, who, even at that time of night, were crawling in and out at the doors, or screaming from the inside."

(*Oliver Twist*, Chapter VIII.)

Letter to Richard Bentley [London, January 24, 1837].

Furnivals Inn.
Tuesday Morning

My Dear Sir.

Oliver Twist making nearly eleven pages, I have only five more to write for the next Miscellany — and those five I am compelled — really compelled; — in such matters, it is not a word that I easily admit into my vocabulary — to defer until some future opportunity, and to make up, as I am carried on by my subject. Mrs. Dickens has been for some days past, in a very low and alarming state; and although she is a little better this morning, I am obliged to be constantly with her, being the only person who can prevail upon her to take ordinary nourishment. I have been labouring for two days past, under a violent attack of God knows what, in the head; and in addition to all my other worry, am experiencing the debility, sickness, and all the other comfortable symptoms consequent upon about as much medicine as would be given to an ordinary-sized horse. Although I have perhaps the best subject I ever thought of, I really cannot write under these combined disadvantages.

If I thought it would injure the next Number, I should find no relief in sitting idle, but it will not, I am certain. I have thrown my whole heart and soul into Oliver Twist, and most confidently believe he will make a feature in the work, and be very popular. The gossip of Lady Mary exceeds our calculation; and without this second paper of mine, the table of contents will be exactly what we agreed upon. I have still a very great deal to do in reading communications, and preparing answers to correspondents; I have done a great deal in altering the papers that will appear, wherever they were weak; and between the one and the other, I really have done, with anxiety and sickness about me, more than nine people out of ten could have performed. We shall have a very strong number, and I am sure you cannot doubt my anxiety and interest in our joint behalf.

Believe me
My Dear Sir
Faithfully Yours
Charles Dickens

Richard Bentley, watching the spectacular rise of "Boz," approached Dickens to become his editor on a new magazine. At first it was to be called *Wits' Miscellany*, but the title was changed to *Bentley's Miscellany*. On November 4, 1836, the agreement was signed for one year, with the first number scheduled for January, 1837. *Oliver Twist* started in the February issue, Part II. It continued until March, 1839. The end of *Pickwick* and the beginning of *Oliver Twist* thus ran simultaneously.

EXTRAORDINARY GAZETTE.

SPEECH OF HIS MIGHTINESS
ON OPENING THE SECOND NUMBER OF
BENTLEY'S MISCELLANY,
EDITED BY "BOZ."

On Wednesday, the first of February, "the House" (of Bentley) met for the despatch of business, in pursuance of the Proclamation inserted by authority in all the Morning, Evening, and Weekly Papers, appointing that day for the publication of the Second Number of the Miscellany, edited by "Boz."

Bentley's Miscellany. Extraordinary Gazette. Inserted at the end of Part III, published on March 1, 1837.

Address.

Twelve months have elapsed since we first took the field, and every successive number of our miscellany has experienced a warmer reception and a more extensive circulation than its predecessor

In the ~~commencing~~ opening of the new year and the ~~commencement~~ of our new volume, we hope to make many changes for the better and none for the worse, and to shew that while we have one grateful eye to past patronage we have another wary one to future favors; in short that like the ~~gossip~~ heroine of the ~~sweet~~ poem descriptive of the faithlessness and flying of Mr John Oakhum of th~~e~~

"Address. 30th November 1837." Manuscript draft.

the Royal Navy, we look
two ways at once.

It is our intention to usher in the
New Year with a very merry meeting, towards
the accomplishment of which end we have
prevailed upon a company of distinguished friends
to mount their hobbies on the occasion, in
humble imitation of those adventurous and
jovial spirits ... their foaming chargers, on
the memorable ninth day of this present
month, while the stones did rattle underneath
as if Cheapside were mad.

These, and a hundred other great designs,
preparations, and surprises are in contemplation, —for the fulfilment of all
of which we are already bound in two volumes
cloth, and have no objection if it
be any additional security to the public, to
stand bound in twenty more.
30th November 1837.

At the end of volume 2, number 12 of *Bentley's Miscellany*, in the December 1, 1837, issue the Editor announced "a hundred other great designs, preparations, and surprises."

As early as September, 1837, disagreement arose between Dickens and Bentley. For Chapman and Hall Dickens was already at work on *Nicholas Nickleby* of which the first number came out in April, 1838. With Bentley *Barnaby Rudge* and the *Memoirs of Joseph Grimaldi* were under discussion. Dickens was overworked and felt that Bentley drew the profit. For three years the duel continued until the editorship of *Bentley's Miscellany* was handed over to William Harrison Ainsworth and Dickens emerged not only completely victorious but with a will forged into a weapon of steel.

Letter to Richard Bentley, [London] September 16, 1837.

48 Doughty Street.
Saturday September 16ᵗʰ 1837.

Sir.

When I left town, I placed a number of accepted articles in the Printer's hands, with directions to set them up in sheets, beginning at the commencement of the number, and to send proofs to me. The whole of this arrangement has been altered by you; proofs of articles which I never saw in Manuscript have been forwarded to me; and notwithstanding my written notice to the Printer that I would revise no such papers, this course has been persisted in, and a second sheet sent.

By these proceedings I have been actually superseded in my office as Editor of the Miscellany; they are in direct violation of my agreement with you, and a gross insult to me. I therefore beg to inform you that henceforth I decline conducting the Miscellany or contributing to it in any way; but in order that you may suffer no inconvenience or embarrassment from the shortness of this notice, I will write a paper this month, and edit the Magazine this month — no longer.

As I feel this course of treatment most strongly, I beg you to understand that it is my firm intention to abide by this determination, regarding the propriety of which, my feeling of what is due to myself, is strengthened by the best advice from others.

I am
Sir,
Yours
Charles Dickens

"*Oliver Twist* was a bold departure from the genial tone of *Pickwick Papers*. Instead of safely echoing the humor and hilarity that had set all England roaring with affectionate laughter, Dickens embarked on a scathing denunciation of the new Poor Law and moved on to a lurid and somber portrayal of London's criminal slums."

(Edgar Johnson, *Charles Dickens*.)

Letter to Charles Edwards Lester, [London] July 19, 1840.

Devonshire Terrace.
Sunday July 19th 1840.

Dear Sir.

As I have not the complete MS of Oliver (I wish I had, as it would one day have an interest for my children) I am enabled to send you a scrap, in compliance with your request; and have much pleasure in doing so.

Pray make my regards to your lady, and give her from me the other little packet inclosed. It is the first specimen of the kind I have parted with — except to a hair-dresser — and will most likely be the last, for if I were to be liberal in this respect, my next portrait would certainly be that of a perfectly bald gentleman.

Believe me Dear Sir
Faithfully Yours
Charles Dickens

P.S. I should tell you perhaps as a kind of certificate of the Oliver scrap, that it is a portion of the original and only draught. — I never copy.

The recipient of Dickens's lock of hair was Ellen, daughter of Capt. Haley Brown, of Sackett's Harbor, New York.

The letter, together with a page of Chapter XV of the original manuscript, was formerly in the possession of another American, Richard Henry Stoddard.

7

Chapter the Tenth

Oliver becomes better acquainted with the characters of his new associates, and purchases experience at a high price. Being a short but very important chapter in his history.

For eight or ten days Oliver remained in the Jew's room, picking the marks out of the pocket handkerchiefs (of which a great number were brought home, already assorted, and sometimes taking part in the game, which the boy and the gentlemen employed regularly every day. At length he began to languish for the fresh air and took many occasions of earnestly entreating the old gentleman to allow him to go out to work with his two companions.

Oliver was rendered the more anxious to be actively employed, by what he had seen of the stern morality of the old gentleman's character. Whenever the Dodger or Charley Bates came home at night empty-handed, he would expatiate with great vehemence on the misery of idle

---

"Chapter the Tenth. Oliver becomes better acquainted with the characters of his new associates . . ."

This is one of three pages given by Dickens to his first cousin, Mrs. Rebecca Ball Wilson.

original Sketch

George Cruikshank

The Last Chance

Oliver Twist; or, The Parish Boy's Progress. London, Richard Bentley, 1838.

The first book to be published under Dickens's own name, *Oliver Twist* appeared in book form six months before it was completed as a serial. Shown above is an original pencil and water color sketch by the illustrator of *Oliver Twist*, George Cruikshank. Entitled "The Last Chance," it became the frontispiece of Volume 3.

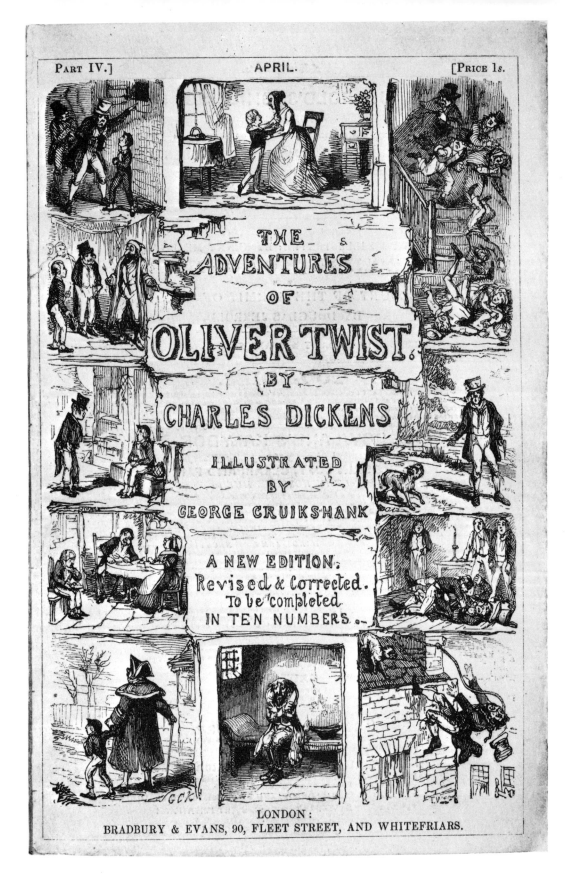

The Adventures of Oliver Twist. Part 1, January-Part 10, October [1846]. London, Bradbury and Evans.

44   This revised edition — the revisions beginning with the title — is exceedingly rare. The illustration above is of Part 4.

George Cruikshank. "Oliver amazed at the Dodger's mode of
going to work." Original pen and ink and water color sketch.

George Cruikshank. "Rose Maylie and Oliver." Original pencil sketch.
Signed by Dickens, probably to signify approval.

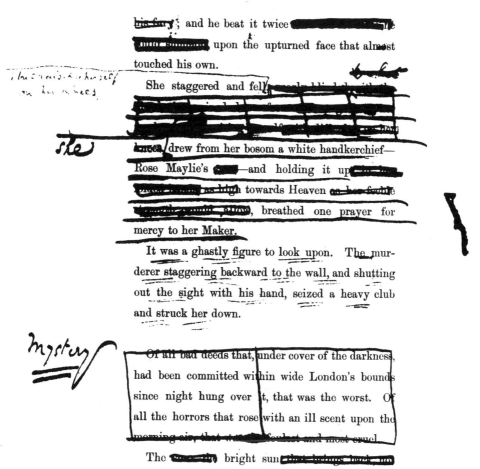

; and he beat it twice ▮▮▮▮▮▮
▮▮▮▮▮▮ upon the upturned face that almost
touched his own.

She staggered and fell ▮▮▮▮▮▮▮▮▮▮▮
▮▮▮▮▮▮▮▮▮▮▮▮▮▮▮▮▮▮▮▮▮▮▮▮
▮▮▮▮▮▮ drew from her bosom a white handkerchief—
Rose Maylie's ▮▮—and holding it up ▮▮▮▮
▮▮▮▮▮▮▮ high towards Heaven ▮▮▮▮▮▮
▮▮▮▮▮▮ ▮▮▮ ▮▮▮▮, breathed one prayer for
mercy to her Maker.

It was a ghastly figure to look upon. The mur-
derer staggering backward to the wall, and shutting
out the sight with his hand, seized a heavy club
and struck her down.

Of all bad deeds that, under cover of the darkness,
had been committed within wide London's bounds
since night hung over it, that was the worst. Of
all the horrors that rose with an ill scent upon the
morning air, that was the foulest and most cruel.

The ▮▮▮▮▮ bright sun ▮▮▮▮▮▮▮▮▮▮

Sikes and Nancy: a Reading from Oliver Twist. [London: Not Published]

This is the only known copy of the privately printed reading edition which served the
actor-author as a prompt copy. Dickens made profuse manuscript changes in the text
and in the margins of his reading copies which accompanied him to his famous lectern.
The conclusion of "Sikes and Nancy" gave Dickens much trouble.

In October, 1868, while engaged in Manchester and Liverpool he wrote to John Forster:
"I have made a short reading of the murder in *Oliver Twist.* I cannot make up my mind, however,
whether to do it or not. I have no doubt that I could petrify an audience by carrying out the
notion I have of the way of rendering it. But whether the impression would not be so horrible as
to keep them away another time, is what I cannot satisfy myself upon."

(*The Letters*, ed. by Walter Dexter, Bloomsbury [London], 1938.)

NEW WORK BY "BOZ."

Messrs. CHAPMAN and HALL have the pleasure of announcing that they have completed arrangements with Mr. CHARLES DICKENS, for the production of an ENTIRELY NEW WORK, to be published monthly, at the same price, and in the same form, as the PICKWICK PAPERS. The first Number will appear on the 31st of March, 1838.

SKETCHES BY "BOZ."

Messrs. CHAPMAN and HALL also beg to announce that they have purchased the entire Copyrights of both Series of these popular Works, for the purpose of enabling the Subscribers to the PICKWICK PAPERS to obtain the whole in one book of the same size, and at the same price. With this view, they purpose publishing the complete collection in Twenty Monthly Numbers, price One Shilling each. The first Number will appear on the 1st of November next, embellished (as will be all its successors) with Two Illustrations, by GEORGE CRUIKSHANK.

186, STRAND,
August 26, 1837.

"New work by 'Boz.'" Announcement in No. 17 of the *Pickwick Papers*, dated August 26, 1837.

In the summer of 1837 Dickens, his wife and Hablôt K. Browne traveled in Flanders — "a hundred places that I cannot recollect now and couldn't spell if I did" — before embarking on *Nicholas Nickleby*. It was to be a vehicle for calling public attention to the horrors of cheap boarding-schools in Yorkshire. In January 1838 Dickens and Browne made the journey in severe winter weather to the locality where schools of the worst repute were situated. Dotheboys Hall with the notorious Wackford Squeers, the proprietor, were so readily identified by the reading public that more than one schoolmaster lay claims to being the original of the prototype. The hero himself, Nicholas Nickleby, was possibly modeled on Dickens's brother-in-law, Henry Burnett.

Letter to Charles Hicks [London, September 20? 1838].

Doughty Street
Thursday Night

Dear Mr. Hicks
    I send you a chapter — 12 pages I hope. You will have another (please God) either on Sunday Night, or Monday Morning. When you have time be good enough to look me up all the old copy you have of mine, as I am very anxious to have it complete.
                    Faithfully Yours
                    Charles Dickens

Charles Hicks was foreman at the printers, Bradbury and Evans.

This letter is the first recorded instance of Dickens's collection of his own manuscripts. Only six chapters of *Nicholas Nickleby* survive.

"Now, the fact was, that both Mr. and Mrs. Squeers viewed the boys in the light of their proper and natural enemies; or, in other words, they held and considered that their business and profession was to get as much from every boy as could by possibility be screwed out of him."

(*Nicholas Nickleby*, Chapter VIII.)

"Whatever I had within me that was romantic and dreamy, was encouraged by so much story-telling in the dark, and in that respect the pursuit may not have been very profitable to me. But the being cherished as a kind of plaything in my room, and the consciousness that this accomplishment of mine was bruited about among the boys, and attracted a good deal of notice to me though I was the youngest there, stimulated me to exertion. In a school carried on by sheer cruelty, whether it is presided over by a dunce or not, there is not likely to be much learnt."

(*David Copperfield*, Chapter VII.)

Letter to Chapman and Hall, [London] January 3, 1839.

48 Doughty Street
Thursday January 3ʳᵈ 1839

Dear Sirs
Will you have the goodness to send in the course of the Day by the Parcels Delivery Company, a set of Nickleby (complete as far as it has gone) directed to Leigh Hunt Esquire 4 Upper Cheyne Row, Chelsea?

Faithfully Yours
Charles Dickens

Dickens began the writing of his story from notes hastily scribbled in Yorkshire. As in the case of *Pickwick* he was never a single number in advance. The work occupied him from February 1838 to October 1839. The "slavery and drudgery" about which he complained to Bentley had to be kept up. Family problems crowded in. On March 6, 1838, a daughter, Mary ("Mamie"), was born and on October 29, 1839, another, Kate Macready Dickens. John Dickens who, after the success of Pickwick, kept asking his son's publishers for loans, was forced into retirement by the author who saw his parents settled in a cottage he found for them near Exeter. Life in the Dickens household was not serene and troubles that started now led to a separation from Kate Dickens twenty years later. It was, however, in November 1839 that the Dickens family moved to the spacious house at No. 1 Devonshire Terrace, Regent's Park, in which Dickens was to spend the happiest years of his life.

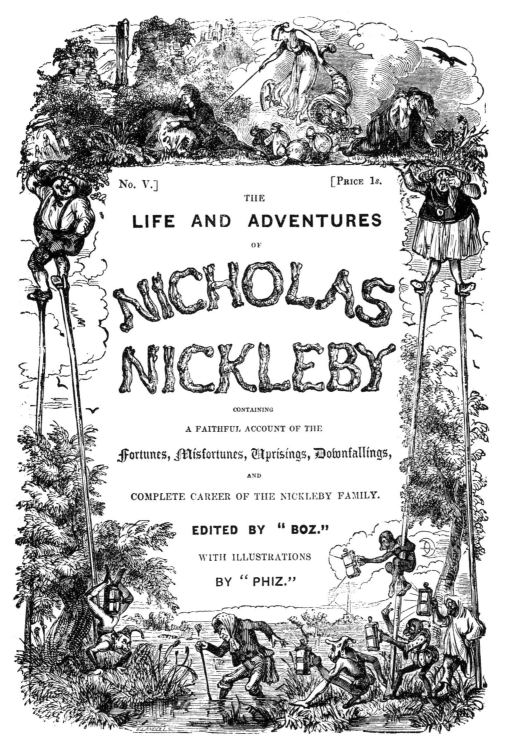

No. V.] [PRICE 1s.

THE

LIFE AND ADVENTURES

OF

NICHOLAS NICKLEBY

CONTAINING

A FAITHFUL ACCOUNT OF THE

Fortunes, Misfortunes, Uprisings, Downfallings,

AND

COMPLETE CAREER OF THE NICKLEBY FAMILY.

EDITED BY "BOZ."

WITH ILLUSTRATIONS

BY "PHIZ."

LONDON: CHAPMAN AND HALL, 186, STRAND.

The Life and Adventures of Nicholas Nickleby. No. 1 [April, 1838]-No. 19-20
[October, 1839]. London, Chapman and Hall.
Shown above is No. 5.

Letter to Clarkson Stanfield [London, October 3, 1839].

Doughty Street
Thursday Morning

My Dear Stanfield.
    On Saturday next, the printers and publishers of the Nickleby, and one or two mutual friends of ours, dine with me at the Albion in Aldersgate Street at 6 for half past precisely to rejoice with me upon the conclusion of the book. Do give me an additional reason for remembering the occasion with pleasure, and join the little party.
Always Faithfully Yours
Charles Dickens

The frontispiece by Daniel Maclise for *The Life and Adventures of Nicholas Nickleby* (London, Chapman and Hall, 1839). The original was presented to Dickens by his publishers. It is now in the National Portrait Gallery and is Dickens's famous likeness. He himself said of it: "Maclise has made another face of me, which all people say is astonishing," and Thackeray called it the real "inward Boz."

Edward Stirling. *Nicholas Nickleby. A Farce in Two Acts. Taken from the popular work of that name by 'Boz.'* As performed at the Royal Adelphi Theatre. London: Published at the National Acting Drama Office.

The illustration is of the wrapper.

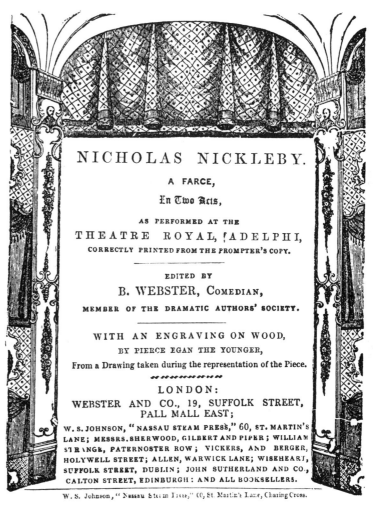

No. 62.

Price 6d.

WEBSTER'S
ACTING NATIONAL DRAMA,
UNDER THE AUSPICES OF THE DRAMATIC AUTHORS' SOCIETY.

NICHOLAS NICKLEBY.

A FARCE,

In Two Acts,

AS PERFORMED AT THE
THEATRE ROYAL, ADELPHI,
CORRECTLY PRINTED FROM THE PROMPTER'S COPY.

EDITED BY
B. WEBSTER, COMEDIAN,
MEMBER OF THE DRAMATIC AUTHORS' SOCIETY.

WITH AN ENGRAVING ON WOOD,
BY PIERCE EGAN THE YOUNGER,
From a Drawing taken during the representation of the Piece.

LONDON:
WEBSTER AND CO., 19, SUFFOLK STREET,
PALL MALL EAST;
W. S. JOHNSON, "NASSAU STEAM PRESS," 60, ST. MARTIN'S
LANE; MESSRS. SHERWOOD, GILBERT AND PIPER; WILLIAM
STRANGE, PATERNOSTER ROW; VICKERS, AND BERGER,
HOLYWELL STREET; ALLEN, WARWICK LANE; WISEHEART,
SUFFOLK STREET, DUBLIN; JOHN SUTHERLAND AND CO.,
CALTON STREET, EDINBURGH: AND ALL BOOKSELLERS.

W. S. Johnson, "Nassau Steam Press," 60, St. Martin's Lane, Charing Cross.

"Long before the final chapters of the story fell into the hands of his readers, a theatrical adapter named Edward Stirling made what Forster terms 'an indecent assault' upon the book; that is to say, he seized upon it, 'hacked, cut, and garbled its dialogue, invented a plot of his own,' and produced it at the Adelphi Theatre. This naturally provoked the indignation of the outraged Author, whose curiosity to witness the performance of so remarkable an adaptation induced him to visit the theatre, at which Forster felt amazed, especially when Dickens praised the making-up and management of certain characters and scenes."

(Frederic G. Kitton, *Charles Dickens.*)

"Yes, sir," ~~said all the little boys with great~~ ~~~~

chuckle

"~~That's right.~~ Keep ready till I tell you to begin. Subdue your appetites, and you've conquered human natur. This is the way we inculcate strength of mind, Mr. Nickleby."

Chuckling

Nicholas murmured something, ~~he knew not~~ ~~what~~ in reply; and the little boys, ~~dividing~~ their gaze between the mug, the bread and ~~butter~~ ~~which had by this time appeared~~; and every morsel ~~which~~ Mr. Squeers took into his mouth, remained ~~with abated breath~~ in torments of expectation.

Wiping mouth

"Thank God for a good breakfast, ~~said Squeers~~ ~~when he had finished~~. Number one may take a drink."

Number one seized the mug ravenously, and had just drunk enough to make him wish for more, when Mr. Squeers gave the signal for number two, who gave up at the ~~most~~ *like* interesting moment to number three; and the process was repeated until the milk and water terminated with number five.

Nicholas Nickleby at the Yorkshire School. A Reading.
Privately Printed.

This is one of two known copies of the privately printed reading edition. Dickens created this text for his second reading tour in 1861-62 in the provincial towns of England. He wrote from Norwich: "I think Nickleby tops all of the readings."

The marginal manuscript instructions reveal the actor and director in Dickens.

Like the other reading copies in the Berg Collection this one was in Dickens's own library at Gad's Hill Place; it bears his bookplate and was bound to his order in red boards with the French peacock pattern.

Hablôt K. Browne ("Phiz"). "The 'Breaking-up' at Dotheboys
Hall," illustration to *Nicholas Nickleby*, Chapter LXIV,
Number XIX-XX. Original pencil and wash sketch.

Letter to John Overs, [London] October 27 [1840].

Devonshire Terrace.
Tuesday 27th October

Dear Mr. Overs.

   First, with regard to the beautiful little model you have sent me, and which I return herewith. The Lion holds in his right paw, a maltese cross, which is made after this manner

✠

— that is to say, so that all the four parts are broad at the base, and go tapering up to the point whence they diverge. Of the present itself, let me assure you that in feeling I have it — complete and perfect in all its parts — and that come when it will, it will be nothing new, or strange, or long in coming, to me.

   Now, with reference to your letter. . .

John Overs, a London cabinet-maker, designed the crest.

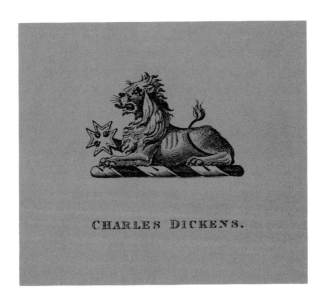

DICKENS'S BOOKPLATE

" 'A lion couchant, bearing in his dexter paw a Maltese cross', as Charles Dickens described it . . . Originally granted in 1625 to William Dickens, citizen of London, the crest's true heraldic description is 'a lion couchant, or in dexter, a cross patonce, sable'. Dickens never recorded a pedigree in the College of Arms nor established his descent from William Dickens. But he used the crest with the Maltese cross for his book-plate . . . on his silver, and on many other possessions; and the crest with the true 'cross patonce' on the china dinner service specially painted for him by Copeland."

(*The Letters*, ed. by Madeline House and Graham Storey, Vol. 2, Oxford, 1969.)

Letter to Richard Bentley [London, October 30, 1837].

Doughty Street
Monday Evening

My Dear Sir.

Lady Blessington's desultory thoughts I have retained. I see nothing likely to be of the slightest service to us in any of the accompanying books, and as I received them all <u>from you</u>, I send them back <u>to you</u>.

I also return the Grimaldi MS. I have thought the matter over, and looked it over, too. It is very badly done, and is so redolent of twaddle that I fear I cannot take it up on any conditions to which you would be disposed to accede. I should require to be ensured three hundred pounds in the first instance without any reference to the Sale — and as I should be bound to stipulate in addition that the work should never be published in Numbers, I think it would scarcely serve your purpose.

I have given out some copy for Wilson to get on with. I shall be at the Old Ship Hotel at Brighton for a week, and any letter will find me there in case you have anything to communicate.

I am
My Dear Sir
Faithfully Yours
Charles Dickens

Joseph Grimaldi, the famous clown, died in May 1837. His friend, Thomas Egerton Wilks, the journalist, took it upon himself to edit Grimaldi's *Memoirs*. His manuscript was bought by Bentley who, in turn, signed an agreement with Dickens in November 1837 to act as editor. What ensued was bitterness on the part of Dickens and a poor publication, brought out by Bentley in 1838.

Letter to Richard Bentley [London, November 23? 1837].

Doughty Street.
Thursday Morning

My Dear Sir

I forward you the draft agreement you sent me, and the draft of another agreement which I propose in lieu, which I think you will find not to differ materially from yours except in respect to the time of payment. If you could see half the offers that lie in my desk at this moment for the employment of the next three or four months, you would deem this a very reasonable alteration. If you cannot accede to these emendations, there is no harm done and Grimaldi can stand upon his own head as he has often done before.

I am very much obliged to you for the books, which are a handsome and most acceptable present. I wish you would oblige me by calling at Laurence's the Portrait Painter's. It would gratify him exceedingly, and I should like you to see his illustrious work.

Faithfully Yours
Charles Dickens.

Samuel Laurence was a popular portraitist of leading writers of the day.

NEW WORK BY "BOZ,"

IN WEEKLY NUMBERS, PRICE THREEPENCE.

NOW WOUND UP AND GOING,

PREPARATORY TO ITS STRIKING,

On Saturday, the 4th of April, 1840,

MASTER HUMPHREY'S CLOCK.

MAKER'S NAME—"BOZ."

THE FIGURES AND HANDS

BY GEORGE CATTERMOLE AND HABLOT BROWNE.

MASTER HUMPHREY earnestly hopes, (and is almost tempted
to believe,) that all degrees of readers, young or old, rich or

Chapman and Hall's Announcement of *Master Humphrey's Clock.*

The plan for this miscellany was announced by the publishers and it was to appear "regularly every Saturday morning." It was to consist of occasional pieces, stories and papers supposedly written by members of a club. A file of these was deposited in the clock. An elderly eccentric, Master Humphrey, was to be the owner. The publication lasted two years, and in it appeared *The Old Curiosity Shop* and *Barnaby Rudge*, both of which were afterwards published separately.

"There is good authority for stating that Dickens derived the name, 'Master Humphrey,' from that of a worthy horologist, William Humphreys, at Barnard Castle, Durham, who, when about sixteen years of age, made the identical timepiece which afterwards became famous as Master Humphrey's Clock."

(Frederic G. Kitton, *Charles Dickens*.)

"Solitary men are accustomed, I suppose, unconsciously to look upon solitude as their own peculiar property."

(*Master Humphrey's Clock*, Part 1, No. 3.)

The November 27 1841 weekly number, and the last monthly part, carried the author's message in closing his work. "Taking advantage of the respite which the close of this work will afford me, I have decided, in January next, to pay a visit to America."

For November 1, 1842, he promised the beginning of a new book in monthly parts. And so "*Master Humphrey's Clock* has stopped for ever."

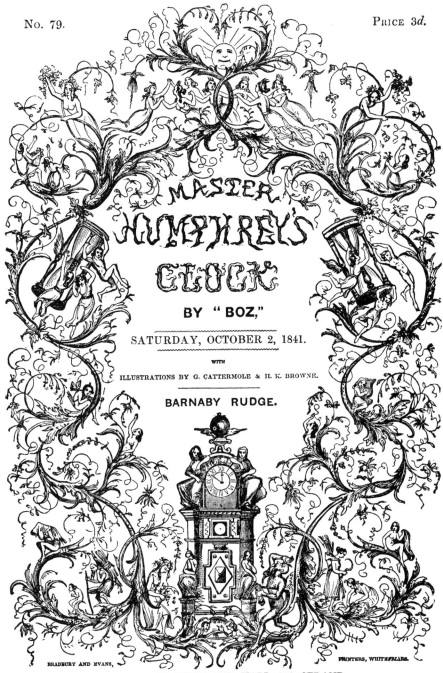

No. 79.   PRICE 3d.

MASTER HUMPHREY'S CLOCK

BY "BOZ,"

SATURDAY, OCTOBER 2, 1841.

WITH

ILLUSTRATIONS BY G. CATTERMOLE & H. K. BROWNE.

BARNABY RUDGE.

BRADBURY AND EVANS,   PRINTERS, WHITEFRIARS.

LONDON: CHAPMAN AND HALL, 186, STRAND;

J. Menzies, Edinburgh; J. Finlay & Co., Glasgow; L. Smith, Aberdeen; S. J. Machen, Dublin; Simms & Dinham, Manchester; Wareing Webb, Liverpool; Wrightson & Webb, Birmingham; S. Simms & Son, Bath; Light & Ridler, Bristol; T. N. Morton, Boston; H. S. King, Brighton; G. Thompson, Bury; E. Johnson, Cambridge; C. Thurnam, Carlisle; J. Lee, Cheltenham; Evans & Ducker, Chester; W. Edwards, Coventry; W. Rowbottom, Derby; W. Byers, Devonport; W. T. Roberts, Exeter; T. Davies, Gloucester; R. Cussons, Hull; Henry Shalders, Ipswich; W. Reeve, Leamington; T. Harrison, Leeds; J. Smith, Maidstone; Finlay & Charlton, Newcastle-on-Tyne, Jarrold & Son, Norwich; R. Mercer, Nottingham; H. Slatter, Oxford; P. R. Drummond, Perth; E. Nettleton, Plymouth; G. Lovejoy, Reading; Brodie & Co., Salisbury; John Innocent, Sheffield; W. Sharland, Southampton; F. May, Taunton; A. Deighton, Worcester; W Alexander, Yarmouth; J. Shillito, York; J. B. Brown, Windsor; and sold by all Booksellers and Newsmen.

Master Humphrey's Clock. No. 1, Saturday, April 4, 1840-No. 88, Saturday, November 27, 1841. London, Chapman and Hall.

The weekly numbers were published in white wrappers. No. 79 is shown here.

Letter to Walter Savage Landor, [London] July 26, 1840.

1 Devonshire Terrace
26th July 1840.

My Dear Landor.

Mr. Shandy's Clock was nothing to mine — wind, wind, wind, always winding am I; and day and night the alarum is in my ears, warning me that it must not run down. When I received that Swing-like letter of yours, such visions of Bath sprung up and floated about me that I rung the bell for my portmanteau and putting it on a chair, looked hard at it for three quarters of an hour. Suddenly a solemn sound from the Clock, jarred upon my ears; and sending it upstairs again, I sat down with a sigh, to write.

Gravely and seriously — for it is a serious matter — I have been looking forward to a glimpse of you were it only for one day, and am still looking forward, and shall be looking forward for Heaven knows how long. I am more bound down by this Humphrey than I have ever been yet — Nickleby was nothing to it, nor Pickwick, nor Oliver — it demands my constant attention and obliges me to exert all the self-denial I possess. But I hope before long to be so far ahead as to have actually turned the corner and left the Printer at the bottom of the next sheet — and then — !

In the meanwhile, when you have the grace to write a long letter I will have the grace to answer it with one of corresponding dimensions, so take care what you do, and what inflictions you call down upon that poetical sconce, on which be all peace and happiness and sunny light for evermore!

BOZ

I was going to put in this place such an effusion (impromptu of course) about her, but as I've only got the first line and the last, and it wants a dozen or so to express the vast idea, I shall defer it until my next, when I shall certainly dispatch it to you. Until then, give her my love, or if you won't — and upon my word I mistrust you — add it to that little private store of your own, and say nothing about it.

Regards to Mrs. Painter and the rest of the family of course. Also to that blighted reed who whispers softly according to the custom of his family and was grown in the softest soil conceivable.

Forster is out of town, but comes home next Wednesday.

At the end of February 1840 Dickens and Forster paid an overnight visit to Landor in Bath. It was during that visit that the form of Little Nell in the old curiosity shop took shape. The young lady mentioned in the letter, Rose Caroline Paynter, introduced Dickens to the original of Quilp, "a frightful little dwarf named Prior, who let donkeys on hire."

"Night is generally my time for walking. In the summer I often leave home early in the morning, and roam about fields and lanes all day, or even escape for days or weeks together, but saving in the country I seldom go out after dark, though, Heaven be thanked, I love its light and feel the cheerfulness it sheds upon earth, as much as any creature living "

(*The Old Curiosity Shop*, Part 1, No. 4.)

PHILADELPHIA
Lea & Blanchard

The Old Curiosity Shop. Philadelphia, Lea & Blanchard, 1841.

This copy of the first American edition was presented by Dickens in person to his American friend Professor Cornelius Felton in New York, on February 23, 1842, with an inscription.

Letter to S. U. Flodell, Gad's Hill Place, May 23, 1868.

> Gad's Hill Place,
> Higham by Rochester, Kent.
> Saturday Twenty Third May, 1868

Dear Sir

I very readily comply with your request proferred through M[r] Dolby, and beg to send you on the other side a short extract, in my writing, from the Old Curiosity Shop.

With many thanks for your attention when I was last in America, and with the assurance of my good will towards you wheresoever I am,

> *Believe me*
> *Faithfully Yours*
> *Charles Dickens*

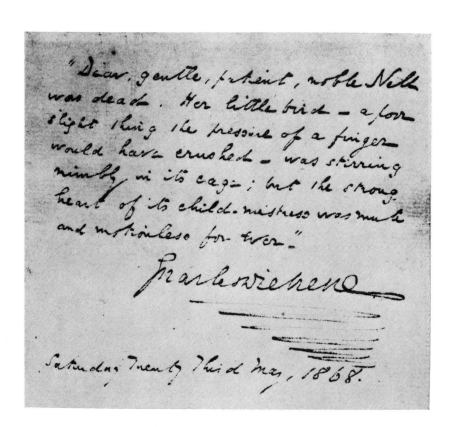

Little Nell commanded everyone's affection. When Dickens decided to "kill her," Thackeray begged him not to. In the United States news of her death was awaited in the harbor. George Dolby, Dickens's American tour manager, seems to have forwarded requests for autographs to Dickens, who in this instance, and counting on Little Nell's popularity, copied out the sentimental lines: "She was dead. Dear, gentle, patient, noble Nell, was dead . . ."

In 1891 an American sculptor, Frank Edwin Elwell, created a bronze statue of Little Nell and Dickens which now stands in Clark Park, West Philadelphia.

George Cattermole. "And thenceforth, every day, and all day long, he waited at her grave for her . . ." Original pen and ink and water color drawing after the wood-engraving on page 216, Part 10, No. 44, *The Old Curiosity Shop*.

Hablôt K. Browne ("Phiz"). ". . . he was conducted to a strong stone cell, where, fastening the door with locks, and bolts, and chains, they left him, well secured . . ."
Original water color drawing after the wood-engraving on page 276, Part 18, No. 76, *Barnaby Rudge*.

Letter to Edward Chapman, [London] March 25 [1840].

Devonshire Terrace
Wednesday 25th. March

My Dear Sir
The best plan will be for Mr. Browne to read the number, and take or make any subject that he fancies. It should have the girl in it, that's all.
Faithfully Yours
Charles Dickens

This refers to Chapter I of *The Old Curiosity Shop* in Part I, published on April 25, in which Little Nell had already been drawn by Cattermole in the headpiece.

Letter to George Cattermole, [London] December 20, 1842.

Devonshire Terrace
Twentieth December 1842

My Dear George
It is impossible for me to tell you how greatly I am charmed with those beautiful pictures, in which the whole feeling and thought and expression of the little story is rendered to the gratification of my inmost heart; and on which you have lavished those amazing resources of yours with a power, at which I fairly wondered when I sat down yesterday before them.
I took them to Mac straightway in a cab — and it would have done you good if you could have seen and heard him. You can't think how moved he was by the old man in the church, or how proud I was to have chosen it, before he saw the drawings.
You are such a queer fellow and hold yourself so much aloof, that I am afraid to say half I would say, touching my grateful admiration. So you shall imagine the rest.
I inclose a note from Kate: to which I hope you will bring the only one acceptable reply.
Always My Dear Cattermole
Faithfully Yours
Charles Dickens

Letter to Charles Gray, [London] October 13, 1840.

> 1 Devonshire Terrace
> York Gate, Regents Park
> 13th October 1840.

Mr. Charles Dickens sends his compliments to Mr. Gray, and if he has no better engagement for next Tuesday, begs the favor of his company to dinner (at Six o'Clock for half past punctually) to meet their fellow-labourers in the Clock, and celebrate the completion of the first Volume.

Charles Gray, engraver and teacher of George Dalziel, engraved Hablôt K. Browne's three illustrations to *Sunday Under Three Heads* and seventy-four of the illustrations to *Master Humphrey*.

Letter to Thomas Hill, [London] October 14 [1840].

> *Devonshire Terrace.*
> *Wednesday 14th October*

My Dear Sir.

Designers, printers, publishers, wood-cutters — in short, the whole of the works of Master Humphrey's Clock dine here next Tuesday at Six for half past exactly, to celebrate the completion of the first Volume. I look upon you as an essential part of the publication; and count surely on your joining us.

I regretted to hear from my brother Fred, that you had not been very well — though I look upon your being anything but well and cheerful, as a sort of practical joke; not an agreeable thing, but still a thing too preposterous to be considered seriously.

> *Always Heartily Yours*
> *Charles Dickens*

Thomas Hill, book-collector and *bon-vivant*, entertained lavishly in his cottage at Sydenham. His parties were known as "the Sydenham Sundays." Shortly after the *Master Humphrey* dinner, on December 20, 1840, he died, leaving behind one of the most copious collections of English poetry in existence.

Letter to Richard Bentley [London, August 17, 1836].

> 15 Furnivals Inn
> Wednesday Evening.

My dear Sir.

I have spoken to some confidential friends, on the subject of our yesterday's Interview. They concur in thinking, and strongly advise me, that for the copyright of a Novel in Three Volumes, I should have Five Hundred Pounds.

I have thought the matter over deliberately: and when I take into consideration, the time, the labour, the casting about, in every direction, for materials: the anxiety I should feel to make it a work on which I might build my fame, and the great probability of it's having a very large sale (we are justified in forming our judgment upon the rapid sale of everything I have yet touched) I think you will not object to raising your terms thus far. I should be very sorry to appear anxious to drive a hard bargain, as nothing is more opposed to my habits and feelings; I confidently believe that on reflection, you will consider I am quite justified in making this request.

If you will think the matter over, between the present time and Monday, I feel quite assured that when I look at the draft of our agreement, on that morning, I shall find that you have adopted my Amendment, and substituted the word "five" for "four". Recollect that you are dealing with an Author not quite unknown, but who, so far as he has gone, has been most successful —

> *Believe me*
> *My Dear Sir*
> *Very faithfully Yours*
> *Charles Dickens*

Barnaby Rudge was discussed as early as 1836. The clash between Dickens and Richard Bentley, one of the most prominent Victorian publishers, seemed inevitable. Amicable relations were resumed in 1857.

Letter to Messrs. Smithson and Mitton, [London] December 16, 1839.

> 1 Devonshire Terrace
> York Gate, Regents Park.
> December 16th 1839

Dear Sirs.

I happened to take up the Morning Herald on Saturday afternoon, and in it saw an advertisement from Mr. Bentley announcing "Mr. Dickens's new work Barnaby Rudge, in three volumes", as "preparing for publication."

I wish you if you please, without delay, formally to make known to Mr. Bentley (through his agents with whom you have already corresponded) what I presume he is already perfectly well acquainted with, through Mr. George Cruikshank — namely, that I am not prepared to deliver the Manuscript of Barnaby Rudge to him on the First of January.

At the same time have the goodness, unless you see some very strong reason to the contrary, to state to those gentlemen why I have placed it out of my power to have the work ready by that time, and why at the present sacrifice of from two to four thousand pounds I prefer leaving Mr. Bentley to avail himself, if he thinks proper, of that penal clause in our agreement (penal as regards me at least) which provides for this contingency.

My chief reason is, that Mr. Bentley in his advertisements and hired puffs of other books with which I never had and never can have any possible connection, has repeatedly within the last four or five months used my name and the names of some of my writings in an un-warrantable manner, dragging them before the public when he had no business to refer to them, and hawking them about in a manner calculated to do me serious prejudice.

When Mr. Bentley first began to publish these repeated allusions, undoubtedly seeking by such means to force the sale of other books by connecting them unfairly with my name, I was at work upon and was progressing rapidly with this Barnaby Rudge. My friends one and all remonstrated with me upon going further; they urged upon me that the publication by Mr. Bentley of a new work of mine under such circumstances would connect me still further with matters with which I have no connection; they pointed out to me how closely Mr. Bentley imitated in external appearance and form of publication everything I did; and left me to judge how fairly he would use my name when he had it, from the manner in which he used it when he had it not. Yielding to these and many like considerations which I need not say nobody can feel so strongly as I, I devoted myself to another work which I had long in contemplation and laid Barnaby Rudge aside.

Since this period Mr. Bentley has published a novel in three volumes at twenty five shillings, and with Heaven knows how many copies on the town, unsold by the booksellers to some of whom they had been delivered but the very day before, republished it immediately, in fifteen weekly parts at a shilling apiece. I have no protection against Mr. Bentley's pursuing exactly the same course in my case; and I neither choose to be considered a party to such proceedings by those who could never know how bound and fettered I should be, nor to arm Mr. Bentley with such a powerful engine of annoyance and injury to my reputation, as a new work of mine would assuredly become in his hands just now.

I therefore take the course which the Agreement distinctly recognizes the possibility of my adopting, and declare that when the specified time arrives, I shall not be prepared with the Manuscript.

I am Dear Sirs
Faithfully Yours
Charles Dickens

Richard Bentley's son, George, later endorsed this letter: "The charges made in this letter, which I bought up, are false. I do not however destroy the letter. It is a brick in the building of Dickens' character. He wished to break his agreement, & so he made up the account contained herein. Dickens was a very clever, but he was not an honest man."

Letter to Angus Fletcher, [London] June 15, 1841.

Devonshire Terrace.
Fifteenth June 1841.

My Dear Fletcher.
Many thanks for your welcome letter.

Ten days let us say — good ten days in the Highlands. But to secure this liberty we must be immoveable in the matter of leaving Edinburgh — stone-steel-adamant. Therefore on the morning of the Saturday week after the dinner, we bolt summarily.

Grip is no more. He was only ill a day. I sent for the medical gentleman (a bird-fancier in the New Road) on the first appearance of his indisposition. He promptly attended, and administered castor oil and warm gruel. Next day, the patient walked in a thoughtful manner up and down the stable till the clock struck Twelve at Noon; then staggered twice; exclaimed "Hal-loa old girl" — either as a remonstrance with his weakness, or an apostrophe to Death: I am not sure which — and expired.

Suspectful of a butcher who had been heard to threaten, I had the body opened. There *were no traces of poison, and it appeared he had died of influenza. He has left a considerable property, chiefly in cheese and halfpence, buried in different parts of the Garden. The new raven (I <u>have</u> a new one, but he is comparatively of weak intellects) administers to his effects, and turns up something every day. The last piece of bijoutrie [sic] was a <u>hammer</u> of considerable size — supposed to have been stolen from a vindictive carpenter who had been heard to speak darkly of vengeance, "down the Mews".*

The medical gentleman, himself — habituated to Ravens — assured me that he "never see sich a thorough going, long-headed, deep, outdacious file" in the whole course of his practice. And he wound up by saying, in reference to Topping "Why, wot was <u>he</u> agin that bird? That 'ere little man could no more stand agin him in pint of sense and reason, than I could agin the ghost of Cobbett".

Good Christians say in such cases "it was all for the best perhaps!" I try to think so, — he had ripped the lining off the carriage and eat the paint off the wheels. In the course of the summer while we were at Broadstairs, I think he would have eat it all, bodily.

I have been fearfully hard at work, morning, noon, and night. I have done now, for the present, and am all impatience to start. — I shall not be quite myself (now that having done I can venture to think of it) until we have taken our first glass of wine at the Royal.

Until when — and always —

> *Believe me Dear Fletcher*
> *Faithfully Yours*
> *Charles Dickens*

I have been greatly importuned by the people of Reading, to stand for the next Parliament, but I can't afford it myself, and I don't choose to be bound hand and foot to the Reform Club. Therefore I don't. Your friend Hall, the Jotter, stands for Taunton. — There is a Heaven above us!

I think it much better that Jeffrey shod. <u>not</u> be in the Chair at the dinner. I dare say he has a delicacy in connection with that. — Wilson is on every ground a better man for the purpose.

Angus Fletcher, the sculptor, was Dickens's guide in Scotland when in Edinburgh midst great celebration the freedom of the city was conferred on the twenty-nine year old writer. The parchment scroll recording the honor hung framed upon his study walls to the end of his life.

Grip the raven, who served as model for his namesake in *Barnaby Rudge*, expired on March 12, 1841.

Letter to William Hall, Broadstairs, September 14, 1841.

> *Broadstairs.*
> *Tuesday Fourteenth Sept.ʳ 1841.*

My Dear Sir.

~~Quite right~~. — Gate of Newgate in 78; not in 79. I don't want Barnaby in the subject, but feared he might be there.

I plainly see that it's all up with the mechanical genius. — Don't trust him with anything; keep an eye on the till; restrain him from making any entries in the books; and unconfuse Mr. Cattermole whom I clearly perceive he will distract with wrong instructions.

I am hideously lazy — always bathing, lying in the sun, or walking about. I write a No. when the time comes, and dream about it beforehand on cliffs and sands — but as to getting in advance — ! where's the use, too, as we soon leave off! —

It would be a good thing, wouldn't it, if I ran over to America about the end of February, and came back, after four or five months, with a One Volume book — such as a ten and six-penny touch? I can't persuade Mrs. Dickens to go, and leave the children at home; or to let me go alone. I wish you'd take an opportunity one of these days, of asking all about the Fares — what a single fare is — what a double fare — what a cabin with child-stowage. I can depend on you, and am afraid to make any enquiries myself, lest it should get blabbed about, before I had quite resolved.

Washington Irving writes me that if I went, it would be such a triumph from one end of the States to the other, as was never known in any Nation. Don't you conceive that it would be, on every account, an excellent employment of a part of the interval? I should like to hear.

When you get the riot-block, will you send me a proof of it?

Faithfully Yours always
Charles Dickens

Letter to Edward Chapman, Broadstairs, September 16, 1841.

Broadstairs
Thursday Sixteenth September 1841.

My Dear Sir.

Know for your utter confusion, and to your lasting shame and ignominy, that the initial letter <u>has</u> <u>been</u> purwided — that it was furnished to the artist at the same time as the sub-ject — that it is a

D

— which stands for Double — Demnible — Doubtful — Dangerous — Doleful — Disastrous — Dreadful — Deuced — Dark — Divorce — and Drop — all applicable to the Precipice on which you stand.

Farewell! If you did but know — and would pause, even at this late period — better an ac-tion for breach than — but we buy experience. Excuse my agitation. I scarcely know what I write. — To see a fellow creature — and one who has so long withstood — still if — Will <u>nothing</u> warn you

In extreme excitement
CD
My hand fails me
Pause
Put it off
P.P.S.
Emigrate
P.P.P.S.
And leave me
the business —
I mean the Strand
one.

On September 22 Chapman married Mary Whiting whose family was Quaker and disapproved of this match. It turned out to be a happy one.

Broadstairs.

Thursday Sixteenth September 1841.

My dear Sir.

Know for your utter confusion, and to your lasting shame and ignominy, that the initial letter has been furnished, that it was furnished to the artist at the same time as the subject — and that it is a

D

— which stands for Double — *Demnible* ~~*various*~~. Dreadful — Dangerous — Doleful — Disastrous. Dreadful — Deuced — Dark — Divorce — and Drop — all applicable to the Precipice on which —you stand.

URING
now at i
fear an
endura·
Wh·
the mu
his, m·
and the struggling of a g·
ear, and, sitting on his b·

The initial letter "D" mentioned in Dickens's letter to Edward Chapman is printed in Chapter 65 of *Barnaby Rudge*. It represents Barnaby and his father awaiting liberation from prison.

Letter to Lewis Gaylord Clark, London, April 14, 1840.

1 Devonshire Terrace, York Gate
Regents Park London
14th April 1840.

My Dear Sir

I am about to write you a very short letter, lest I should despair, in the multitude of my avocations, and write none at all.

Firstly — believe me, that I have not forgotten the promise to the Knickerbocker — that I cannot venture to say when I can redeem my pledge — but that I <u>will</u> redeem it, please Heaven, and strive for an early opportunity. You may suppose that I am very much engaged with Master Humphrey's Clock.

Secondly — commend me heartily to Mr. Washington Irving, who I am rejoiced to hear from you has lent his powerful aid to the international copyright question. It is one of immense importance to me, for at this moment I have received from the American Editions of my works — fifty pounds. It is of immense importance to the Americans likewise if they desire (and if they do not, what people on earth should) ever to have a Literature of their own.

Thirdly — accept my thanks for your kind communications, and a hasty but sincere assurance of the pleasure they afford me, and of the truth with which I am

Faithfully Yours
Charles Dickens

Lewis Gaylord Clark was an editor and author under whose guidance the *Knickerbocker Magazine* became the leading literary journal of its day. He also edited the *Knickerbocker Sketch-Book* to which Washington Irving contributed.

On January 22, 1842, Mr. and Mrs. Charles Dickens landed in Boston. It had been a rough journey, which the travelers privately described in detail to a brother, Frederick Dickens, on January 30th; the author publicly in the opening chapters of his *American Notes*. The couple returned from New York on June 7th. The journey ended in disillusionment: democracy and American morals did not appeal to Dickens at close range. He also fought a battle against the casual approach to copyright. For every friend he made in America he had also made an enemy.

Letter for the American Press, Niagara Falls, April 27, 1842.

To the Editor &c

Sir.

I found, awaiting me yesterday at the Post office in Buffalo, certain letters from England, of which the following are copies. I ask the favor of you that you will publish them in your columns; and I do so in order that the People of America may understand that the sentiments I have expressed on all public occasions since I have been in these United States, in reference to a law of International copyright, are not merely my individual sentiments, but are without any qualification, abatement or reserve, the opinions of the great body of British authors — represented by the distinguished men whose signatures are attached to these documents.

That they are also the opinions of the native writers of America, they have sufficiently shewn in their earnest petitions to the Legislature upon this subject.

I would beg to lay particular stress upon the letter from Mr Carlyle; not only because the plain and manly Truth it speaks is calculated, I should conceive, to arrest attention and respect in any country, and most of all in this; but because his creed in this respect is, without the abatement of one jot or atom, mine; and because I never have considered and never will consider this question in any other light than as one of plain Right or Wrong — Justice or Injustice.

I am Sir
Your faithful Servant
Charles Dickens

Niagara Falls.
  Twenty Seventh April 1842

To The American People.

We the undersigned, in transmitting to one of our most eminent English authors the following memorial for an International Copyright between the United States and Great Britain, are willing that our claims should be considered apart from our interests in urging them.

Addressing a Great Nation chiefly united to us by a common ancestry . . .

In October 1842 Dickens published his travel notes: *American Notes for General Circulation.* (In two volumes. London, Chapman and Hall, 1842.) The book was dedicated to those friends of his in America "who, giving [him] a welcome [he] must ever gratefully and proudly remember." On October 18th he inscribed a copy (now in the Berg Collection) to one such friend, Sir Richard Jackson, who on his arrival in Montreal on May 11th sent his four-in-hand for Dickens to welcome him "in grand style."

"It would be well, there can be no doubt, for the American people as a whole, if they loved the real less and the ideal somewhat more. It would be well, if there were greater encouragement to lightness of heart and gaiety, and a wider cultivation of what is beautiful, without being eminently and directly useful."

(*American Notes*, Chapter XVIII.)

Check drawn on the Baltimore bankers, Robert Gilmer and Son, for $500, dated Cincinnati, April 5, 1842.

Dickens liked Cincinnati. He wrote to Forster: ". . . a very beautiful city, I think the prettiest place I have seen here except Boston."

Letter to Frederick Dickens [Boston, January 30, 1842].

My Dear Fred.

You were quite right, and may retire from public life upon an honorable independence, as soon as you please. Hewett <u>did</u> stand upon the paddle-box — with a brazen speaking trumpet in his hand — wherewith he gave his orders to the men, which were passed by sundry officers in handsome naval uniforms, from one to another, until they reached the required point. You should see the engines of one of these large vessels. There are thirty men, who attend to them alone. The sea ran so high all the way, that when we came into Boston, the funnel which was properly red, was <u>white</u> to the top with the ocean's salt. Such a battered looking ship as it was, you can hardly imagine. When we put into Halifax, the fragments of our Nolan life boat still hung upon the deck. The rumour ran from mouth to mouth, that we had picked up the wreck of one of the poor President's boats at sea; and the crowd came down for splinters of it, as valuable curiosities!

I was ill for 5 days — Kate for 6. After that time we managed our knives and forks with great credit to ourselves and expense to the Cunard Company. In Winter time, and with such heavy weather, it is a most miserable voyage — wretched and uncomfortable beyond all description.

I can't tell you what they do here to welcome me, or how they cheer and shout on all occasions — in the streets — in the Theatres — within doors — and wherever I go. But Forster holds the papers I have sent him, in trust to communicate this news to everybody. I have only time to write one letter, which is anything like a letter. He has it, and will tell you all.

We leave here on Saturday, and go with the Governor to a place called Worcester where we stay all Sunday. On Monday we go to a place called Springfield, and there we are publicly met by the citizens of Hartford, and carried on to that place: where — on Wednesday — I have a public dinner. On Thursday, I have another public reception at Newhaven — on Saturday, we reach New York. On Monday they give me a great ball there, the committee for which alone is 150 strong. In the same week a great public dinner, and [tear] a dinner with a club. I believe this is to go on all through the States. You may say [tear] I have not much time to spare.

I have engaged a very good and modest secretary, who lives with us when we travel, and has ten dollars a month. He does his work very well, and I like him much.

God bless you and the darling children.
I long to be at home.
Always your affectionate brother
CD

I inclose the Ginirit's receipts. As Park saw us on board, will you call upon him — remember me to him — say I had no time to write before the packet left — and tell him all the news? Will you do the same by Stanfield, <u>without loss of time</u>?

The "very good and modest secretary" mentioned in this letter was George W. Putnam to whom Dickens also gave his "Letter to the Editor" on copyright for sending out to the American press.

Letter to Edgar Allen Poe, [Philadelphia] March 6, 1842.

> United States Hotel
> Sixth March 1842

My Dear Sir

I shall be very glad to see you, whenever you will do me the favor to call. I think I am more likely to be in the way between half past eleven and twelve, than at any other time.

I have glanced over the books you have been so kind as to send me; and more particularly at the papers to which you called my attention. I have the greater pleasure in expressing my desire to see you, on their account.

Apropos of the "construction" of Caleb Williams. Do you know that Godwin wrote it _backwards_ — the last volume first — and that when he had produced the hunting-down of Caleb, and the catastrophe, he waited for months, casting about for a means of accounting for what he had done?

> Faithfully Yours always
> Charles Dickens

Edgar Allan Poe, then the editor of *Graham's Magazine*, wrote a review of *Barnaby Rudge* and predicted the plot of the story.

Letter to Albany Fonblanque, Washington, March 12, 1842.

> Washington (Fuller's Hotel)
> Twelfth March 1842.

My Dear Fonblanque.

I have reserved my fire upon you until I came to this place, thinking you would best like to know something about the political oddities of this land. No doubt you have heard the leading points in my adventures — as how we had a bad passage out, of 18 days — how I have been dined, and balled (there were 3000 people at the ball) and feted in all directions — and how I can't stir, without a great crowd at my heels — and am by no means in my element, in consequence. I shall therefore spare you these experiences, whereof Forster is a living chronicle; and carry you straightway to the President's house.

It's a good house to look at, but — to follow out the common saying — an uncommon bad 'un to go; at least I should think so. I arrived here on Wednesday night; and on Thursday morning was taken there by the Secretary to the Senate: a namesake of mine, whom "John Tyler" had despatched to carry me to him for a private interview which is considered a greater compliment than the public audience. We entered a large hall, and rang a large bell — if I may judge from the size of the handle. Nobody answering the bell, we walked about on our own account, as divers other gentlemen (mostly with their hats on, and their hands in their pockets) were doing, very leisurely. Some of them had ladies with them to whom they were shewing the premises; others were lounging on the chairs and sofas; others yawning and picking their teeth. The greater part of this assemblage were rather asserting their supremacy than doing anything else; as they had no particular business there, that anybody knew of. A few were eyeing the moveables as if to make quite sure that the President (who is not popular) hadn't made away with any of the furniture, or sold the fixtures for his private benefit.

After glancing at these loungers who were scattered over a pretty drawing room, furnished with blue and silver, opening upon a terrace with a beautiful prospect of the Potomac river and adjacent country – and a larger state room, not unlike the dining room at the Athenaeum – we went up stairs into another chamber, where were the more favored visitors who were waiting for audiences. At sight of my conductor, a black in plain clothes and yellow slippers, who was moving noiselessly about, and whispering messages in the ears of the more impatient, made a sign of recognition and glided off to announce us.

There were some twenty men in the room. One, a tall, wiry, muscular old man from the West, sunburnt and swarthy, – with a brown white hat and a giant umbrella, who sat bolt upright in his chair, frowning steadily at the carpet, as if he had made up his mind that he was going to "fix" the President in what he had to say, and wouldn't bate him a grain. Another, a Kentucky farmer nearly seven feet high, with his hat on, and his hands under his coat tails, who leaned against the wall, and kicked the floor with his heel, as though he had Time's head under his shoe, and were literally "killing" him. A third, a short, round-faced man with sleek black hair cropped close, and whiskers and beard shaved down into blue dots, who sucked the head of a big stick, and from time to time took it out of his mouth to see how it was getting on. A fourth did nothing but whistle. The rest balanced themselves, now on one leg, and now on the other, and chewed mighty quids of tobacco – such mighty quids, that they all looked as if their faces were swoln [sic] with erisypelas. They all constantly squirted forth upon the carpet, a yellow saliva which quite altered its pattern; and even the few who did not indulge in this recreation, expectorated abundantly.

In five minutes time, the black in yellow slippers came back, and led us into an upper room – a kind of office – where, by the side of a hot stove, though it was a very hot day, sat the President – all alone; and close to him a great spit box, which is an indispensable article of furniture here. In the private sitting room in which I am writing this, there are two; one on each side of the fire place. They are made of brass, to match the fender and fire irons; and are as bright as decanter stands. – But I am wandering from the President. Well! The President got up, and said, "Is <u>this</u> Mr Dickens?" – "Sir," returned Mr Dickens – "it is." "I am astonished to see so young a man Sir," said the President. Mr Dickens smiled, and thought of returning the compliment – but he didn't; for the President looked too worn and tired to justify it. "I am happy to join with my fellow citizens in welcoming you, warmly, to this country," said the President. Mr Dickens thanked him, and shook hands. Then the other Mr Dickens, the secretary, asked the President to come to his house that night, which the President said he should be glad to do, but for the pressure of business, and measles. Then the President and the two Mr Dickenses sat and looked at each other, until Mr Dickens of London observed that no doubt the President's time was fully occupied, and he and the other Mr Dickens had better go. Upon that they all rose up; and the President invited Mr Dickens (of London) to come again, which he said he would, and that was the end of the conference.

From the President's house, I went up to the Capitol, and visited both the Senate, and the House of Representatives, which as I dare say you know are under one roof. Both are of the amphitheatre form, and very tastefully fitted up; with large Galleries for ladies, and for the public generally. In the Senate, which is much the smaller of the two, I made the acquaintance of everybody in the first quarter of an hour – among the rest of Clay, who is one of the most agreeable and fascinating men I ever saw. He is tall and slim, with long, limp, gray hair – a good head – refined features – a bright eye – a good voice – and a manner more frank and captivating than I ever saw in any man, at all advanced in life. I was perfectly charmed with him. In the other house, John Quincy Adams interested me very much. He is something like Rogers, but not so infirm; is very accomplished; and perfectly "game." The rest were in appearance a good deal like our own Members — some of them very bilious-looking, some very rough, some heartily good natured, and some very coarse. I asked which was Mr Wyse, who lives in my mind, from the circumstance of his having made a very violent speech about England t'other day, which he emphasized (with great gentlemanly feeling and good taste) by pointing, as he spoke, at Lord Morpeth who happened to be present. They pointed out a wild looking, evil-visaged man, something like Roebuck, but much more savage, with a great ball of tobacco in his left cheek. I was quite satisfied.

I didn't see the honorable member who on being called to order by another honorable member some three weeks since, said "Damn your eyes Sir, if you presume to call <u>me</u> to order, I'll cut your damnation throat from ear to ear;" — he wasn't there — but they shewed me the honorable member to whom he addressed this rather strong Parliamentary language; and I was obliged to content myself with him.

Yesterday, I went there again. A debate was in progress concerning the removal of a certain postmaster, charged with mal-practises, and with having interfered in elections. The speaking I heard, was partly what they call "stump oratory" — meaning that kind of eloquence which is delivered in the West, from that natural rostrum — and partly, a dry and prosy chopping of very small logic with very small mincemeat. It was no worse than ours, and no better. One gentleman being interrupted by a laugh from the opposition, mimicked the laugh, as a child would in quarrelling with another child, and said that "before he had done he'd make honorable members sing out, a little more on the other side of their mouths." This was the most remarkable sentiment I heard, in the course of a couple of hours.

I said something just now, about the prevalence of spit-boxes. They are everywhere. In hospitals, prisons, watch-houses, and courts of law — on the bench, in the witness box, in the jury box, and in the gallery; in the stage coach, the steam boat, the railroad car, the hotel, the hall of a private gentleman, and the chamber of Congress; where every two men have one of these conveniences between them — and very unnecessarily, for they flood the carpet, while they talk to you. Of all things in this country, this practice is to me the most insufferable. I can bear anything but filth. I would be content even to live in an atmosphere of spit, if they would but spit <u>clean</u>; but when every man ejects from his mouth that odious, most disgusting, compound of saliva and tobacco, I vow that my stomach revolts, and I cannot endure it. The marble stairs and passages of every handsome public building are polluted with these abominable stains; they are squirted about the base of every column that supports the roof; and they make the floors brown, despite the printed entreaty that visitors will not disfigure them with "tobacco spittle." It is the most sickening, beastly, and abominable custom that ever civilization saw.

When an American gentleman is polished, he <u>is</u> a perfect gentleman. Coupled with all the good qualities that such an Englishman possesses, he has a warmth of heart and an earnestness to which I render up myself hand and heart. Indeed the whole people have most affectionate and generous impulses. I have not travelled anywhere yet, without making upon the road a pleasant acquaintance who has gone out of his way to serve and assist me. I have never met with any common man who would not have been hurt and offended if I had offered him money, for any trifling service he has been able to render me. Gallantry and deference to females are universal. No man wo^d retain his seat in a public conveyance to the exclusion of a lady, or hesitate for an instant in exchanging places with her, however much to his discomfort, if the wish were but remotely hinted. They are generous, hospitable, affectionate, *and kind. I have been obliged to throw open my doors at a certain hour, in every place I have visited, and receive from 300 to 7 or 800 people; but I have never been asked a rude or impertinent question, except by an Englishman — and when an Englishman has been settled here for ten or twelve years he is worse than the Devil.*

For all this, I would not live here two years — no, not for any gift they could bestow upon me. Apart from my natural desire to be among my friends and to be at home again, I have a yearning after our English customs and English manners such as you cannot conceive. It would be impossible to say, in this compass, in what respects America differs from my preconceived opinion of it, but between you and me — privately and confidentially — I shall be truly glad to leave it, though I have formed a perfect attachment to many people here, and have a public progress through the Land, such as it never saw, except in the case of Lafayette. I am going away now, into the Far West. A public entertainment has been arranged in every town I have visited; but I found it absolutely necessary to decline them — with one reservation. — I am going now, to meet a whole people of my readers in the Far West — two thousand miles from N. York on the borders of the Indian Territory!

Since I wrote the inclosed sheet, I have had an Invitation from the President to dinner. I couldn't go: being obliged to leave Washington before the day he named. But Mrs Dickens and I went to the public drawing room where pretty nearly all the natives go, who choose. It was most remarkable and most striking to see the perfect order observed — without one soldier, sailor, constable, or policeman in attendance, within the house or without; though the crowd was immense.

I have been as far South, as Richmond in Virginia. — I needn't say how odious the sight of Slavery is, or how frantic the holders are in their wrath against England, because of this Creole business. — If you see Forster soon, ask him how the Negroes drive in rough roads.

And if you should ever have time to scratch a few lines to a poor transported man, address them to the care of David Colden Esquire 28 Laight Street, Hudson Square, New York. He will forward them to me wherever I be. You must do on your side, what I can't do on this — pay the postage — or your letter will come back to you.

How long will the Tory Ministry last? Say six months, and receive my blessing.

Mrs Dickens unites with me in best regards to Mrs Fonblanque and her sister.

And I am always — My Dear Fonblanque
Faithfully Your friend
Charles Dickens

Albany Fonblanque was a journalist who made contributions mainly to the *Morning Chronicle* and the *Examiner*. The editorship of the latter passed to Dickens's friend, John Forster, hence Fonblanque's friendship with Dickens.

The manuscript of the above letter to Fonblanque is illustrated on the following pages.

Washington (Fuller's Hotel)

Twelfth March 1842.

My Dear Fonblanque.   I have reserved my fire upon you until I came to
this place, thinking you would best like to know something about the political
oddities of this land. No doubt you have read the leading points in my adventures — as how we had a bad passage out, of 18 days — how I have been dined, and
balled (there were 3000 people at the ball) and feted in all directions — and
how I can't stir, without a great crowd at my heels — and am by no means in
my element, in consequence. I shall therefore spare you these experiences, whereof
Forster is a living chronicle; and carry you straightway, to the President's house.

It's a good house to look at, but — to follow out the common saying —
an uncommon bad 'un to go; at least I should think so. I arrived here on
Wednesday night; and on Thursday morning was taken there by the Secretary
to the Senate: a namesake of mine, whom "John Tyler" had despatched to
carry me whither for a private interview which is considered a greater compliment than the public audience.   We entered a large hall, and rang
a large bell — if I may judge from the size of the handle. Nobody answering
the bell, we walked about on our own account, as divers other gentlemen (most
with their hats on, and their hands in their pockets) were doing, very leisurely.
Some of them had ladies with them to whom they were shewing the premises;
others were lounging on the chairs and sofas; others, yawning and picking
their teeth. The greater part of this assemblage were rather asserting
their supremacy, than doing anything else; as they had no particular business
there that anybody knew of.   A few were eyeing the moveables as if
to make quite sure that the President (who is not popular) hadn't made
away with any of the furniture, or sold the pictures for his private benefit.

After glancing at these loungers who were scattered over a pretty
drawing room, furnished with blue and silver, opening upon a terrace with a
thankful prospect of the Potomac river and adjacent country — and a larger
state room, not unlike the dining room at the athenaeum — we went up
stairs into another chamber, where the more favored visitors who were waiting
for audiences, were making at sight of my conductor, a black

in plain clothes and yellow slippers, who was moving noiselessly about, and whispering messages in the ears of the more impatient, made a sign of recognition and glided off to announce us.

There were some twenty men in the room. One, a tall, wiry, muscular old man from the West, sunburnt and swarthy, with a brown white hat and a giant umbrella, who sat bolt upright in his chair, pouring steadily at the carpet, as if he had made his mind up that he was going to "fix" the President in what he had to say, and wouldn't bate him a grain. Another, a Kentucky farmer nearly seven feet high, with his hat on, and his hands under his coat tails, who leaned against the wall, and kicked the floor with his heel, as though he had Time's head under his shoe, and were literally "killing" him. A third, a short, round-faced man with sleek black hair cropped close, and whiskers and beard shaved down into blue dots, who sucked the head of a big stick, and from time to time took it out of his mouth to see how it was getting on. A fourth did nothing but whistle. The rest balanced themselves, now on one leg, and now on the other, and chewed mighty quids of tobacco - such mighty quids, that they all looked as if their faces were swoln with erysipelas. They all constantly squirted forth upon the carpet, a yellow saliva which quite altered its pattern; and even the few who did not indulge in this recreation, expectorated abundantly.

In five minutes' time, the black in yellow slippers came back, and led us into an upper room - a kind of office - where, by the side of a hot stove, though it was a very hot day, sat the President - all alone; and close within a peat, spit box, which is an indispensable article of furniture here. In the private sitting room in which I am writing this, there are two; one on each side of the fire place. They are made of brass, to match the fender and fire irons; and are as bright as decanter stands. But I am wandering from the President. Well! the President got up, and said, "Is this Mr. Dickens?" - "Sir," returned Mr. Dickens, "it is." "I am astonished to see so young a man, sir," said the President. Mr. Dickens smiled, and thought of returning the compliment - but he didn't; for the President looked too worn and tired, to justify it. "I am happy to join with my fellow citizens in welcoming you warmly, to this country," said the President. Mr. Dickens thanked him, and shook hands. Then the other Mr. Dickens, the secretary, asked the President to come to his house, that night, which the President said he should be glad to do, but for the pressure of business and measles. Then the President and the two Mr. Dickens sat and looked at each other, until Mr. Dickens of London observed that no doubt the President's time was fully occupied, and he and the other Mr. Dickens had better go. Upon that they all rose up; and the President invited Mr. Dickens (of London) to come again, which he said he would, and that was the end of the conference.

From the President's house, I went up to the Capitol, and visited both the Senate, and the House of Representatives, which as I dare say you know are under one roof. Both are of the amphitheatre form, and very tastefully fitted up; with large galleries for ladies, and for the public generally. In the Senate, which is much the smaller of the two, I made the acquaintance of everybody in the first quarter of an hour—among the rest of Clay, who is one of the most agreeable and fascinating men I ever saw. He is tall and slim, with long, limp, grey hair—a good head—refined features—a bright eye—a good voice—and a manner more frank and captivating than I ever saw in any man, at all advanced in life. I was perfectly charmed with him. In the other house, John Quincy Adams interested me very much. He is something like Rogers, but not so infirm; is very accomplished; and perfectly "game". The rest were in appearance a good deal like our own members—some of them very bilious-looking, some very rough, some heartily good natured, and some very coarse. I asked which was Mr Wise, who lives in my mind, from the circumstance of his having made a very violent speech about England t'other day, which he emphasized (with great gentlemanly feeling and good taste) by pointing, as he spoke, at Lord Morpeth who happened to be present. They pointed out a wild looking, evil-visaged man, something like Roebuck, but much more savage, with a great ball of tobacco in his left cheek. I was quite satisfied.

I didn't see the honorable member who one thing called Wander & another honorable member something three weeks since, said "Damn your eyes Sir, if you presume to call me to order, I'll cut your damnation throat from ear to ear;"—he wasn't there—but they shewed me the honorable member to whom he addressed this rather strong Parliamentary language; and I was obliged to content myself with him.

Yesterday, I went there again. A debate was in progression concerning the removal of a certain postmaster, charged with mal-practices and with having interfered in elections. The speaking I heard, was partly what they call "stump oratory"—meaning that kind of eloquence which is delivered in the West, from that natural rostrum—and partly, a dry and chopping of very small logic into very small mincemeat. It was no worse than ours, and no better. One gentleman being interrupted by a laugh from the opposition, mimicked the laugh, as a child would in quarrelling with another child, and said that "before he had done he'd make honorable members sing out, a little more on the other side of their mouths." This was the most remarkable sentiment I heard, in the course of a couple of hours.

I said something just now, about the prevalence of spit-boxes. They are everywhere. In hospitals, prisons, watch-houses, and courts of law — on the bench, in the witness box, in the jury box, and in the gallery; in the stage coach; the steam boat, the railroad car, the hotel, the hall of a private gentleman, and the chamber of Congress; where every two men have one of these conveniences between them — and very unnecessarily, for they flood the carpet, while they talk to you. Of all things in this country, this practice is to me the most insufferable. I can bear anything but filth. I would be content even to live in an atmosphere of spit, if they would but spit clean; but when every man spits from his mouth that odious most disgusting compound of saliva and tobacco, I vow that my stomach revolts, I cannot endure it. The marble stairs and passages of my handsome public building are polluted with these abominable stains; they are squirted about the base of every column that supports the roof; and they make the floors brown, despite the printed entreaty that visitors will not disfigure them with "tobacco spittle". It is the most sickening, beastly, and abominable custom that our civilization saw.

When an american gentleman is polished, he is a perfect gentleman coupled with all the good qualities that such an englishman possesses, has a warmth of heart and an earnestness to which I make up myself hand and heart. Indeed the whole people have most affectionate and generous impulses. I have not travelled anywhere yet, without making upon the road a pleasant acquaintance who has gone out of his way to serve and assist me. I have never met with any common man who would not have been hurt and offended if I had offered him money for any trifling service he has been able to render me. Gallantry and deference to females are universal. No man retains his seat in a public conveyance to the exclusion of a lady, or hesitates for an instant in exchanging places with her, however much to his discomfort, if the wish were but remotely hinted. They are generous, hospitable, affectionate and kind. I have been obliged to throw open my doors at a certain hour, in every place I have visited, and receive from 300 to 7 or 800 people; but I have never once been asked an impertinent or unpertinent question, except by an englishman — and when an englishman has been settled here for ten or twelve years, he is worse than the Devil. For all this, I would not live here two years — no, not for an gift they conned us for upon me. Apart from my natural desire to be among my friends and to be at home again, I have a yearning after our English customs and English manners such as you cannot conceive. It would be impossible to say, in this compass, in what respects America differs from my preconceived opinion of it, but between you and me—privately and confidentially. I shall be truly glad to leave it, though I have formed a perfect attachment to many people here, and have a public progress through the land, such as it never saw, except in the case of Lafayette. I am going away now into the far west. A public entertainment has been arranged in every town I have visited; but I found it absolutely necessary to decline them—with one reservation.—I am going now, to meet a whole people of my readers in the far west—two thousand miles from N. York—on the borders of the Indian Territory!

Since I wrote the inclosed sheet, I have had an invitation from the President to dinner. I couldn't go: being obliged to leave Washington before the day he named. But Mrs Dickens and I went to the public drawing room where pretty nearly all the nation's go, who choose. It was most remarkable and most striking to see the perfect order observed—without one soldier, sailor, constable, or policeman in attendance, within the house or without; though the crowd was immense.

I have been as far south, as Richmond in Virginia.—I needn't say how odious the sight of slavery is, or how rankly the holders are in their wrath against England, because of this creole business.—If you see Forster soon, ask him how the negroes drive in rough roads.

And if you should ever have time to scratch a few lines to a poor transported man, address them to the care of David Colden Esquire 28 Laight Street, Hudson Square, New York. He will forward them to me wherever I am. You must do on your side, what I can't do on this—pay the postage, or your letter will come back to me.

How long will the Tory ministry last? Say six months, and receive my blessing.

Mrs Dickens unites with me in best regards to Mrs Fonblanque and her sister. And I am always, My dear Fonblanque

Faithfully Your friend
CHARLES DICKENS

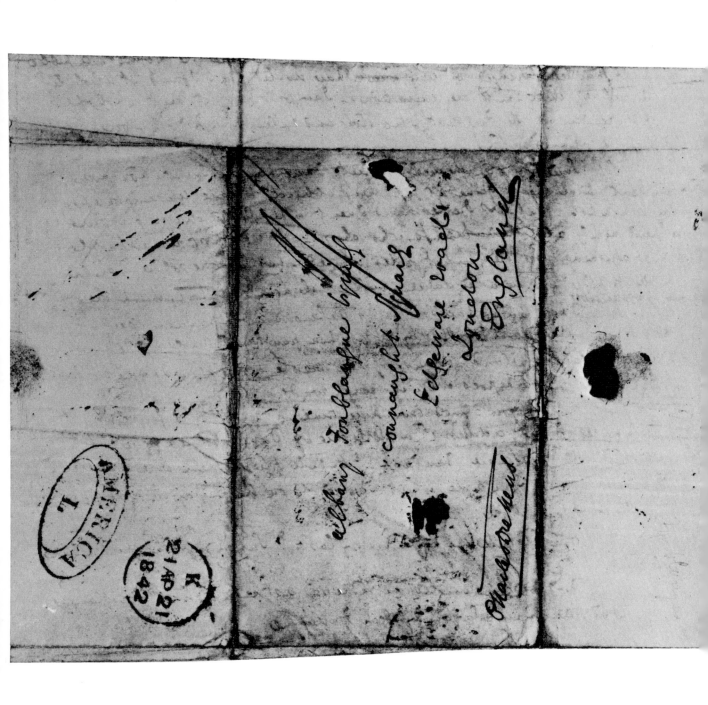

Letter to Washington Irving, [Washington] March 15, 1842.

Fuller's
Fifteenth March 1842.

My Dear Irving.

We leave here tomorrow night. — Say that you will come and dine with us tomorrow — inviolably alone — at 4. Don't refuse, if you love me. It may be a very long time before we dine together again.

I am glad to say that I have a brother to whose memory we can drink a glass of wine — he died in his infancy some nine and twenty years ago. He wasn't a twin, but we must make the best of him.

Heartily Your friend
Charles Dickens

Washington Irving and Charles Dickens shared many a joke and had many good laughs together. Dickens had visited Irving at Sunnyside; in Washington, where, partly because of Kate Dickens's illness and partly because of the climate, Dickens was not happy, Irving was the companion he wanted most.

Letter to Mrs. Frances Trollope, [London] December 16, 1842.

Devonshire Terrace
York Gate Regents Park
Sixteenth December 1842

My Dear Mrs Trollope

Let me thank you most cordially for your kind note in reference to my notes; which has given me true pleasure and gratification.

As I never scrupled to say in America, so I can have no delicacy in saying to you, that allowing for the change you worked in many social features of American society, and for the time that has passed since you wrote of the country, I am convinced that there is no writer who has so well and accurately (I need not add, so entertainingly) described it, in many of its aspects, as you have done; and this renders your praise the more valuable to me.

I do not recollect ever to have heard or seen the charge of exaggeration made against a feeble performance, though in its feebleness, it may have been most untrue. It seems to me essentially natural and quite inevitable, that common abusers should accuse an uncommon one of this fault, and I have no doubt that you were long ago of this opinion; very much to your comfort.

Mrs. Dickens begs me to thank you for your kind remembrance of her: and to convey to you, her best regards.

Always believe me,
Faithfully Yours,
Charles Dickens

Frances Trollope, novelist and writer of travel books, had sailed to the United States in 1827, where she spent twenty-five months in frontier Cincinnati and sixteen months of extreme poverty in the eastern United States. After her return to England, she published in 1832 her *Domestic Manners of the Americans*, thus preceding Dickens's *American Notes* by a decade.

Letter to Cornelius Mathews, [London] December 28, 1842.

> *1 Devonshire Terrace, York Gate*
> *Regents Park*
> *Twenty Eighth December 1842*

My Dear Sir

I was very glad to receive your letter, and to read your remarks on the spirit of the American book. I know it deserves them for its good intentions.

Do not suppose, I beg you, that I for a moment misunderstood your suggestions in reference to the want of an International copyright, or that I conceived it possible you had any personal or private interest to serve, in making them. I simply intended to convey to you my rooted and decided objection to get the better of the nefarious system which now exists (and will, long after you and I are dead) by an <u>evasion</u>, or to take anything from the American People which they will not give me honestly and openly. So far as I am concerned, your intensely intelligent and respectable newspapers shall have the full credit and profit of the present state of things, and perhaps, in time, your publishers may begin to see that it is to their interest to have some Law beside the Law of Plunder.

I have to thank you for the copy of Puffer Hopkins you have kindly sent me for myself; and to acknowledge the receipt of those other sheets of the same work which you sent me at the same time for a purpose, to which, I am sorry to say, I cannot put them. I know of no publisher here, who is at all disposed to reprint an American book unless it have attached to it, some name which is already well known on this side of the water. Since I came home, I have, in the discharge of other commissions to the same effect, several times offered American books (on any terms) to Mr. Moxon, the most likely bookseller for the purpose; but always with the same result.

In the matter of the Brother Jonathan, I would certainly recommend you to take charge of that Journal, if you can do so with profit and advantage. As to your using the works of British authors, there can be no doubt that you would be justified in doing so, while matters remain as they are; and that the best return you could make would be the advocacy of an honorable and honest change. At the same time, I am quite certain in my own mind that such an advocacy would seriously affect its circulation, when opposed to the free and independent doctrines of Mr. Benjamin: which are popular and patriotic.

> *My Dear Sir*
> *Faithfully Yours*
> *Charles Dickens*

Cornelius Mathews was a regular contributor to the *Knickerbocker Magazine* and with his friend E. A. Duyckinck founder of the monthly, *Arcturus*.

Letter to Martin Farquhar Tupper, Brighton, March 19, 1850.

Brighton, Nineteenth March 1850.

My Dear Sir

I am extremely gratified by the terms in which you address me. Your letter is most welcome to me, and has given me the utmost pleasure. Now, as a reader of yours, (though I could wish you had given me more to do) [1] *have all kinds of pleasant and interesting associations with* <u>you</u>. *And hence the uncommon satisfaction I have in your genial consideration of me.*

I shall not remain here many days longer, and shall be delighted to see you in town if you will propose a time that will suit your convenience. My engagements (of business) are so very numerous just now, that I fear I am not at all likely to make a burst into your part of the country, yet awhile.

When I went to America, I did <u>not</u> take my children, though I took my wife. We had not such an amazing caravan then, as we have now, but I left them at home.

I am perfectly acquainted, however, as you may suppose, with every kind of accommodation and want of accommodation in travelling, all over the States, as well as on the Voyage. I will take the last, first.

Most decidedly, no steamer will take you for anything like the money you name. And I have not the shadow of a shade of a doubt — as Brougham says — that you ought to go in a Liner: i e a packet ship. There is infinitely more room; you can make room, by knocking two "state rooms" into one (as I did coming home); you can construct for your whole family without difficulty, for almost half a steamer's charges; the motion is incomparably easier; the interest of the passage much greater; you might even take the whole of the Ladies cabin, and be in a perfect house of your own. Against all these advantages, you have merely to set a longer passage. But I apprehend time to be less important to you than comfort; and the sea-sickness once over (mind! You would not be half so sick in an airy, skimming ship, as in a mad, plunging Sea-Bull of a steamer, bent on rushing head first at any demoniacal obstacle that is to be found in the Atlantic, and going through the water instead of over it) another week or two is a mere luxurious idleness. I expect to see the Captain of the finest Packet Ship in this trade, on Sunday next. I will sound him closely about all the Ships; knowing him to be one of the most honest and skilful mariners in the world. The result of our discourse shall be yours when you please.

If you have <u>two</u> servants accustomed to children, on whom you can thoroughly depend, I would recommend you to take them. An American Help is a tremendous misnomer, even in an American case. But in an English case! — I should say Mrs. Tupper would go mad in a month.

There would be a Cow aboard ship. (I mean that for C. O. W.) The steward would tell you, in connection, whether you would require, with that milk-consuming band, any tins besides.

The children would be as hearty aboard ship as under any circumstances in the world. Few packet ships carry Surgeons. Take a medicine chest. Surgeons in the steamers.

I cannot think of any place in America where I would like to leave my children, they being strangers to the air and soil, so well as at Boston or in the neighborhood of Boston; or at, or near, Hartford in Connecticut. In the latter place, they would be more in your way (I don't mean as incumbrances) when you were travelling about, than in the former. But if I contemplated such a move, I should almost be inclined to leave mine in Canada — at King-

ston or Montreal — surrounded by English. There are delightful people among the Americans — more simple-hearted and good natured than almost any I know — but it would be an extraordinarily strange thing to a lady, to find herself alone for months together, in a little American town. Boston *always* excepted. And supposing you sailed to New York, you would very easily take them there. New York would not do — much too feverish.

I shall be very happy to give you any amount of details you may ask for. Generally, this is what occurs to me in answer to your questions. I believe, I am quite "up" in the subject in all its branches. Either to Boston or to Canada, I could give you letters that would help to make M*rs* Tupper happy, and at home.

Believe me
My Dear Sir
Very faithfully Yours
Charles Dickens

Tupper gained great popularity in America with his *Proverbial Philosophy*, 1838, with which he was thought "to have eclipsed Solomon." His American and Canadian "Ballads" also promoted international kindliness. In 1851 and 1876 he was enthusiastically welcomed in the United States.

Since the return from America, his wife's sister, Georgina Hogarth, had become part of his household, of which she remained a member until his death; and he had just reason to be proud of the steadiness, depth, and devotion of her friendship. In a note-book begun by him in January, 1855, where for the first time in his life he jotted down hints and fancies proposed to be made available in future writings, is a character sketched of which the most part was applicable to his sister-in-law, if the whole was not suggested by her.

"She sacrificed to children, and sufficiently rewarded. From a child herself, always 'the children' (of somebody else) to engross her. And so it comes to pass that she never has a child herself — is never married — is always devoted 'to the children' (of somebody else), and they love her — and she has always youth dependent on her 'till her death — and dies quite happily.' "

(John Forster, *Forster's Life of Dickens.*
Abridged and revised by George Gissing.)

Mems:

The unwieldy ship, taken in Tow by the snorting little steam Tug. [Done in Copperfield and Pecksniff?]

The drunken? — dissipated? — what? —
— Lion, and his Jackall and Primer — stealing down whence at unmixed hours. [Done in Carton]

"The office." The life of the office. The men in it.

Our house. Whatever it is, it is in a first-rate situation and a fashionable neighbourhood. (auctioneer called it "a gentleman's residence.") a series of little closets squeezed up into the corner of a dark street — but a Duke's mansion round the corner. The whole house just large enough to hold a vile smell. The air breathed in it at the best of times, a kind of Distillation of Mews. [Done in the Tetterbys?]

"Ships Buying, so poor, shabby — father? — a new hat. So incongruous that it makes him like African King Boy, or King George is himself full dressed in a cocked hat or a waistcoat — and nothing else.

The man who invariably says opposite things (in the new

"Memoranda. January 1855." Memorandum book with Dickens's manuscript entries for possible use in his work.

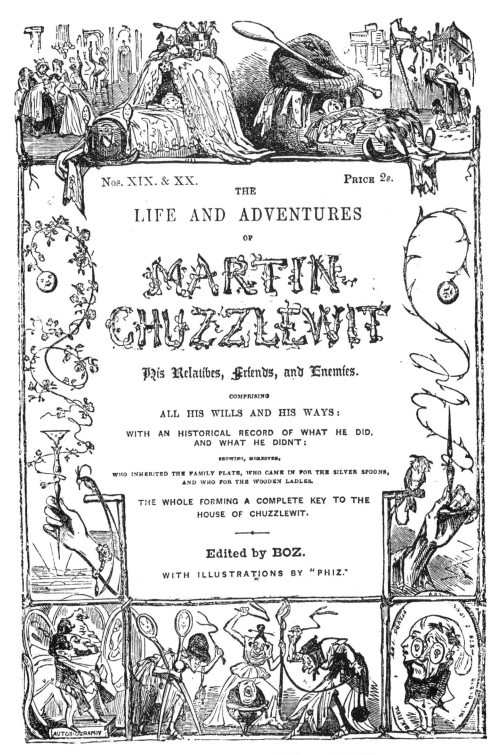

Nos. XIX. & XX.

PRICE 2s.

THE

LIFE AND ADVENTURES

OF

MARTIN CHUZZLEWIT

His Relatives, Friends, and Enemies.

COMPRISING

ALL HIS WILLS AND HIS WAYS:

WITH AN HISTORICAL RECORD OF WHAT HE DID,
AND WHAT HE DIDN'T:

SHOWING, MOREOVER,

WHO INHERITED THE FAMILY PLATE, WHO CAME IN FOR THE SILVER SPOONS,
AND WHO FOR THE WOODEN LADLES.

THE WHOLE FORMING A COMPLETE KEY TO THE
HOUSE OF CHUZZLEWIT.

Edited by BOZ.

WITH ILLUSTRATIONS BY "PHIZ."

LONDON: CHAPMAN & HALL, 186, STRAND.

July 1844.

The Life and Adventures of Martin Chuzzlewit. No. 1, January,
1843-No. 19-20, July, 1844. London, Chapman and Hall.
The last number is illustrated here.

Hablôt K. Browne ("Phiz"). "Illustrations to Martin Chuzzlewit." One of a series of forty original water color drawings, prepared in 1866 for the collector Frederick William Cosens.

" 'Here's this morning's New York Sewer!' cried one. 'Here's this morning's New York Stabber! Here's the New York Family Spy! Here's the New York Private Listener! Here's the New York Peeper! Here's the New York Plunderer! Here's the New York Keyhole Reporter! Here's the New York Rowdy Journal! Here's all the New York papers! Here's full particulars of the patriotic loco-foco movement yesterday, in which the whigs was so chawed up; and the last Alabama gouging case; and the interesting Arkansas dooel with Bowie knives; and all the Political, Commercial, and Fashionable News. Here they are! Here they are! Here's the papers, here's the papers!' "

(The Life and Adventures of Martin Chuzzlewit, Chapter XVI.)

THE

LIFE AND ADVENTURES

OF

MARTIN CHUZZLEWIT.

———◆———

BY CHARLES DICKENS.

The Life and Adventures of Martin Chuzzlewit.
London, Chapman and Hall, 1844.

This copy of the first issue of the first edition in book form was presented by Dickens to Thomas Chapman, the Chairman of Lloyds, who has been described as the original of Mr. Dombey of *Dombey and Son*.

In *Martin Chuzzlewit* "Pecksniff, himself, was unquestionably drawn from a miscellaneous writer and editor, S. C. Hall – 'Shirtcollar Hall', Douglas Jerrold used to call him – and, to leave no doubt, he was introduced in the novel as: 'A most exemplary man . . . His very throat was moral. You saw a good deal of it. You looked over a very low fence of white cravat . . . and there it lay, a valley between two jutting heights of collar, serene and whiskerless before you.' Whether Hall ever specifically did anything to earn Dickens's disapproval is unknown."

(K. J. Fielding, *Charles Dickens; a Critical Introduction.*
Second edn., London, 1965.)

Letter to George Henry Lewes, Broadstairs, August 11, 1847.

Broadstairs
Eleventh August 1847.

My Dear Lewes

The delay has arisen in my desire to accept Giles Homespun's invitation (honest Man!) and in my casting about for a way of doing so. But I haven't found it – after more trials than you have any idea of – for I am hard and fast here, until October. Not with work alone (that I could do in Staffordshire) but with family visitors and other bedevilments of that nature, which perplex a man who has had the misfortune in infancy to pray for the welfare of a great many relations and friends.

I enclose a note for Giles. I shouldn't wonder if he were to ask me again, at some odd time or another.

I am at a great loss for a means of blowing my superfluous steam off, now the play is over – but that is always my misfortune – and find myself compelled to tear up and down, between this and London, by express trains. The little book descriptive of the Amateur Theatricals is nearly done. It is written by Mrs Gamp and inscribed to Mrs Harris. It seems that Mrs Gamp, hearing of the expedition, and being informed that several of the ladies attached to it were in various stages of an interesting state, accompanied it, unbeknown, in a second cladge [i.e. class] carriage, on the chance of being called in.

I wonder she wasn't – seeing that Mrs Leech was taken ill at the London station [&] wheeled to the Victoria Hotel in a Bath chair – and there confined triumphantly. She was in my carriage; so I was a witness to the seizure and the wheeling. She is a capital little woman, and I am glad its over.

From any future personal participation in such achievements, may the humble individual who now addresses you (father of seven young children) be himself delivered!

Ever Yours
Charles Dickens

I am reading Ranthorpe with great interest and pleasure.
More of that, anon.

George Henry Lewes, philosophical writer and first editor of the *Fortnightly Review*, was a close friend of Dickens.

"Both in structure and in vividness of character portrayal, *Martin Chuzzlewit* reveals Dickens in the fullness of his powers. Nevertheless, although not an absolute failure with the public, it met with the poorest reception of any of his novels. Nor is the reason hard to find. Dickens had returned from America with a grimmer gaze for human shortcomings than he had taken there."

(Edgar Johnson, *Charles Dickens*.)

Although Dickens broke off his relationship with Chapman and Hall at the expiration of his contract and did not resume business with his old friends for thirteen years, *Martin Chuzzlewit* went through many editions. His publishers by contract for the ensuing eight years were to be Messrs. Bradbury and Evans.

"In 1847 Dickens entertained the idea of reviving Mrs. Gamp by writing in her peculiar vernacular a little *jeu d'esprit* in the form of a history of a theatrical tour organized by himself and friends (Cruikshank, Leech, Mark Lemon, &c.), for the purpose of raising a fund for the benefit of Leigh Hunt; but this literary joke perished prematurely when only a few pages of manuscript had been prepared."

(Frederic G. Kitton, *Charles Dickens*.)

Shown opposite is a page from the only known copy of the privately printed reading edition. "Mrs. Gamp", the reading, culled by Dickens from several chapters of *Martin Chuzzlewit*, occupies 53 printed pages. Dickens's manuscript additions and deletions indicate the many changes he made in his role as actor while reading in public between 1858 and 1868 about this tipsy nurse.

Like other reading copies that served as his manuscript in composing his readings, this one was bound for Dickens and bears his bookplate.

" Why did he die before his poor old, crazy servant ! " ████████████████ Take him from me, and what remains ? I loved him. He was good to me. ████████████████████████ I took him down once, six boys, in the arithmetic class*at school*, God forgive me ! Had I the heart to take him down ! "

████████████████████████████████
████████████████████████████████
████████████████████████████████
████████████████████████████████
████████████████████████████████

" Well, I 'm sure," said Mrs. Gamp, ~~looking~~ *blessed* ~~hard at him~~ ; " you 're a wearing old soul, and that 's the ~~sacred~~ truth. It 's a pity you don't know wot you say, for you 'd tire your own pagienge out if you did, and fret yourself into a happy releage for all as knows you ; ████████████████████

You ought to know that you was born in a wale, and that you live in a wale, and that you must take the consequences of sich a sitiwation

The Poor Traveller: Boots at the Holly-Tree Inn: and Mrs. Gamp.
London, [Privately printed by Bradbury and Evans], 1858.

"Such a bustle ensued that you might have thought a goose the rarest of all birds; a feathered phenomenon, to which a black swan was a matter of course — and in truth it was something very like that in that house. Mrs. Cratchit made the gravy (ready beforehand in a little saucepan) hissing hot; Master Peter mashed the potatoes with incredible vigour; Miss Belinda sweetened up the apple-sauce; Martha dusted the hot plates; Bob took Tiny Tim beside him in a tiny corner at the table; the two young Cratchits set chairs for everybody, not forgetting themselves, and mounting guard upon their posts, crammed spoons into their mouths, lest they should shriek for goose before their turn came to be helped. At last the dishes were set on, and grace was said."

(*A Christmas Carol*, Stave Three.)

"Who can listen to objections regarding such a book as this? It seems to me a national benefit, and to every man or woman who reads it a personal kindness. The last two people I heard speak of it were women; neither knew the other, or the author, and both said, by way of criticism, 'God bless him!' "

(William Makepeace Thackeray, "A Box of Novels."
In *Fraser's Magazine*, February, 1844.)

"There is no doubt that, by reason of his little Christmas Books, Dickens had distinctly identified himself with the festive season, to which he thus imparted a touch of joviality and good-feeling of the old-fashioned English kind, so much so that the omission of a Yule-tide story, around which his magic pen could weave such delightful fancies, was regarded as a real public loss."

(Frederic G. Kitton, *Charles Dickens.*)

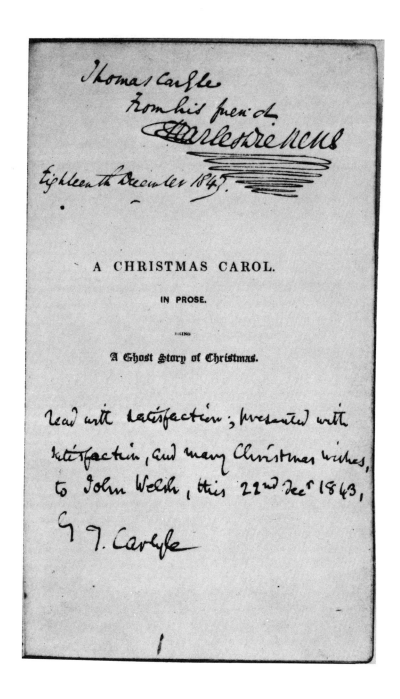

A Christmas Carol. London, Chapman & Hall, 1843.

Dickens presented this copy to Thomas Carlyle, with an inscription, on December 18, 1843. Four days later a relative of Mrs. Jane Welsh Carlyle, John Welsh, received this same copy reinscribed by Carlyle: "read with satisfaction; presented with satisfaction, and many Christmas wishes . . ."

Letter to Cornelius Felton, London, January 2, 1844.

Devonshire Terrace London
Second January 1844.

My very dear Felton.

You are a Prophet, and had best retire from business straightway. Yesterday morning, New Year's Day, when I had walked into my little work room after breakfast and was looking out of [the] window at the snow in the Garden — not seeing it particularly well in conse-quence of some staggering suggestions of last night's Punch and Turkey, whereby I was be-set — the Postman came to the door with a knock for which I damned him from my heart. Seeing your hand upon the corner of a letter which he brought, I immediately blessed him — presented him with a glass of whiskey — enquired after his family (they are all well) — and opened the dispatch, with a moist and oystery twinkle in my eye. And on the very day from which the New Year dates, I read your New Year congratulations, as punctually as if you lived in the next house. — Why don't you!

Now, if instantly upon the receipt of this, you will send a free and independent citizen down to the Cunard wharf at Boston, you will find that Captain Hewett of the Britannia Steam Ship (my ship) has a small parcel for Professor Felton of Cambridge; and in that par-cel you will find a Christmas Carol in Prose. Being a Ghost Story of Christmas by Charles Dickens. Over which Christmas Carol, Charles Dickens wept, and laughed, and wept again, and excited himself in a most extraordinary manner in the composition; and thinking where-of, he walked about the black streets of London, fifteen and twenty miles, many a night when all the sober folks had gone to bed. He don't like America, I am told, but he has some friends there, as dear to him as any in England; so you may read it safely. Its success is most prodigious. And by every post, all manner of strangers write all manner of letters to him about their homes and hearths, and how this same Carol is read aloud there and kept on a very little shelf by itself. Indeed it is the greatest success as I am told, that this ruffian and rascal has ever achieved.

Forster is out again — and if he don't go in again after the manner in which we have been keeping Christmas, he must be very strong indeed. Such dinings, such dancings, such con-jurings, such blindmans buffings, such theatre-goings, such kissings-out of old years and kissings-in of new ones, never took place in these parts before. To keep the Chuzzlewit going, and do this little book, the Carol, in the odd times between two parts of it, was, as you may suppose, pretty tight work. But when it was done, I broke out like a madman. And if you could have seen me at a children's party at Macreadys the other night, going down a country dance (something longer than the Library at Cambridge) with Mrs M. you would have thought I was a country Gentleman of independent property, residing on a tip-top farm, with the wind blowing straight in my face every day.

We have not yet achieved that family performance I told you of; which I expect will come off in the course of next week. Kate is not quite as well as usual: being nervous and dull. But her health is perfectly good, and I am sure she might rally, if she would. I shall be much relieved when it is well over. In the mean time total abstinence from oysters seems to be the best thing for me; and good spirits for all of us. She is much rejoiced to hear that Mrs Felton continues to improve; and sends her cordial love. In which I, no less cordially, join.

Your friend Mr. Parker dined with us one day (I don't know whether I told you this, be-fore?), and pleased us very much. Mr Coleman has dined here once, and spent an evening here. I have not seen him lately, though he has called twice or thrice; for Kate being unwell, and I busy, we have not been visible at our accustomed seasons. I wonder whether Hamlet has ever fallen in your way. Poor Hamlet! He was a good fellow, and has the most grateful heart I ever met with. Our journeyings with Hamlet, seem to be a dream, now. Talking of dreams, strange thoughts of Italy and France — and maybe Germany — are springing up within me, as the Chuzzlewit clears off. It's a secret I have heardly breathed to anyone, but I "think" of leaving England for a year, next midsummer — bag and baggage, little ones and all — then coming out with _such_ a story, Felton — all at once — no parts — sledge hammer blow.

I send you a Manchester paper, as you desire. The report is not exactly done, but very well done, notwithstanding. It was a very splendid sight, I assure you, and an awful-looking audience. I am going to preside at a similar meeting at Liverpool on the 26th of next month; and on my way home, I may be obliged to preside at another at Birmingham. I will send you papers, if the reports be at all like the real thing.

Forster thought I should be very much surprised by what you told him of Lardner; but I was not. I don't know much of the man — but I know the country he is in, and think he acted with great sagacity.

I wrote to Prescott about his book, with which I was perfectly charmed. I think his descriptions, masterly; his style, brilliant; his purpose, manly and gallant always. The introductory account of Aztec civilization impressed me, exactly as it impressed you. From beginning to end, the whole History is enchanting and full of Genius. I only wonder that having such an opportunity of illustrating the Doctrine of Visible Judgments, he never remarks when Cortes and his men tumble the Idols down the Temple steps and call upon the people to take notice that their Gods are powerless to help themselves — that possibly if some intelligent native had tumbled down the Image of the Virgin or patron Saint after them, nothing very remarkable might have ensued, in consequence.

Of course you like Macready. Your name's Felton. I wish you could say [sic] him play Lear. It is stupendously terrible. But I suppose he would be slow to act it, with the Boston company.

Hearty remembrances to Sumner, Longfellow, Prescott, and all whom you know I love to remember. Countless happy years to you and yours, my dear Felton, and some instalment of them, however slight, in England, in the loving company of

The Proscribed One.

oh breathe not his name.

The copy inscribed to Felton, and dated by Dickens "New Year's Day 1844", is now in the Berg Collection.

"The family performance" referred to was the birth of Dickens's fifth child, Francis Jeffrey Dickens, who arrived on January 15th and died in America in 1886.

"Hamlet" is George W. Putnam, who acted as Dickens's secretary in America.

William Hickling Prescott's _History of the Conquest of Mexico_ was published in 1843.

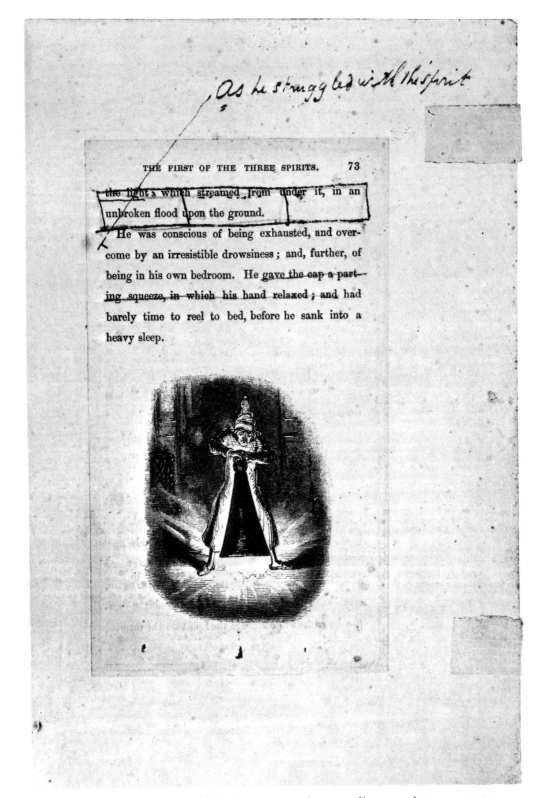

As he struggled with the spirit

THE FIRST OF THE THREE SPIRITS. 73

the light which streamed from under it, in an unbroken flood upon the ground.

He was conscious of being exhausted, and overcome by an irresistible drowsiness; and, further, of being in his own bedroom. He gave the cap a parting squeeze, in which his hand relaxed; and had barely time to reel to bed, before he sank into a heavy sleep.

A Christmas Carol. Twelfth edition. London, Bradbury and Evans, 1849.

Dickens's own copy, from which he gave his public readings, with his bookplate and library binding. From the first reading of the *Carol*, on December 27, 1854, delivered at the Town Hall in Birmingham in aid of the new Midland Institute, to its last performance on March 15, 1870, which was Dickens's Farewell Reading, Dickens the author and actor shared with his audience the thrill of hearing the *Carol*. By 1864 he had perfected, in the copy shown here, the final version for his act.

Letter to Thomas Mitton, [London] February 10, 1844.

Devonshire Terrace
Tenth February 1844

My Dear Mitton.

Fred was telling me last night about the impudence of the Pirates — which I think I had much better not know, unless they should give us an opportunity of being [sic] down upon them in some new fashion. For I can easily conceive the possibility of its being an advantage to us, and certainly a position of dignity, to be able to declare that I have never seen their effusions. Even in the event of your thinking it desirable at any time that I should be acquainted with their doings, I should like to receive the book sealed up, that I might even then pause before I looked into it.

Have you seized the second man, and has the first appeared? It seems to me that we have no course but to go on with the action pell mell. It is of no use to falter with such rascals.

Mr. Blanchard's name is not Laman at all. He was christened Eduard Lyt, and is a desperate bad character. I can get the certificate of his christening. Jerrold knows all about him.

Mr. Cleare, I also find, is active in the business. I have set the real Blanchard to get news of him, and think I shall be able to trail the "gent."

On we must go. Depend upon that.

C and H promise the Carol accounts, today.

Faithfully Always
CD

This letter refers to a piracy of *A Christmas Carol* appearing in *Parley's Illuminated Library*. The legal action Dickens took drove the pirates into bankruptcy. Thomas Mitton, solicitor and one of Dickens's oldest friends, received the original manuscript of *A Christmas Carol* as a gift from the author. Today it is one of the treasures of The Pierpont Morgan Library.

Letter to Frederick Dickens, Albaro, [Genoa] July 22, 1844.

Villa Di Bagnerello. Albaro.
Monday Twenty Second July 1844.

My Dear Fred.

    I have written a rather long letter to Mitton, with a few wandering notes of this place, which I have begged him to put you in possession of, forthwith, and as I dare say you will have heard from Forster besides, I will confine myself at this moment, to what immediately concerns you — namely, the notion you had of coming here, in your holidays. I am assured that the journey, straight through, can be very well done in something less than a week; for £15 each way. If you should decide to come, I will very gladly stand £10 of this Thirty. And I can answer for your seeing all manner of novelties, and being very much entertained in this New World. — I believe (but I will enquire further into this, if you decide to come) that you would cross the Alps, and not steam it. In that case; or indeed in any, most probably; I would come on to some point to meet you. Such French phrases as you would want, I could give you in a letter; but you can book yourself to Paris, in London; and very nearly to this place, in Paris. And one word "combien" — how much? — would carry you further than you are likely to go, in Foreign Parts.

    Let me know what you really intend in this respect; and [tear] can make all that part of it, easy enough, if you decide to come.

    We are all very well, Thank God; and living in the queerest [tear] of place that ever was anywhere. We expect a Piano up from Genoa to-day. I [treated?] the Pigs with a carriage yesterday, wherein they went to that city, with Roche, Cook, and the Nurses; and seeing a very magnificent religious Procession in the streets, came back with a decided leaning towards the roman Catholic faith. The Genoese ladies wear veils instead of bonnets, and we had no rest here, until the Dolls were similarly attired.

    Fletcher is living with us, and desires to be heartily remembered. He says "Boots" are cheap here; and you can't do better than come and buy 'em. But I don't know what you would do on the pavements; which are very trying. It is like walking on marbles, with here and there a peg-top — all red hot and smoking.

    Kate, Georgy, and the darlings, send their loves. Give mine to everybody who comes in your way, who is worth receiving it. Address still to the Poste restante, Genoa, as that is the shortest mode. If Mitton gives you the MS of the last 2 No^s of Chuzzlewit, will you give it to Forster.

                    Your affectionate Brother
                    Charles Dickens

P.S. Will you see Topping
      one evening, and ascertain
      that the Phaeton had
      come home, safely?

"Early in September, Dickens went to Marseilles to meet his brother Fred, who was coming to pass a fortnight's holiday at Genoa. They made the return journey over the Alps and along the Corniche Road, resting overnight at inns resembling ancient wine vaults and infested with mosquitoes and 'fleas of elephantine dimensions . . . gambolling boldly in the dirty beds.' "

(Edgar Johnson, *Charles Dickens.*)

Dickens and his family lived in Italy from July, 1844, to June, 1845. First in a suburb of Genoa, then in the rented Palazzo Peschiere, Dickens wrote weekly letters to Forster; his second Christmas story, *The Chimes*; entertained friends and family; and it was from Genoa that he visited Venice, Verona, Mantua and Rome — places described in a book for which Samuel Palmer designed vignettes.

Upon his return Dickens accepted the editorship of the *Daily News*. The preliminary number of January 21, 1846, carried the first installment of *Pictures from Italy* under the title "Travelling Letters — Written on the Road." The printed book contained five additional chapters.

The copy illustrated is inscribed to the actor John Pritt Harley, Dickens's friend from youthful theatricals.

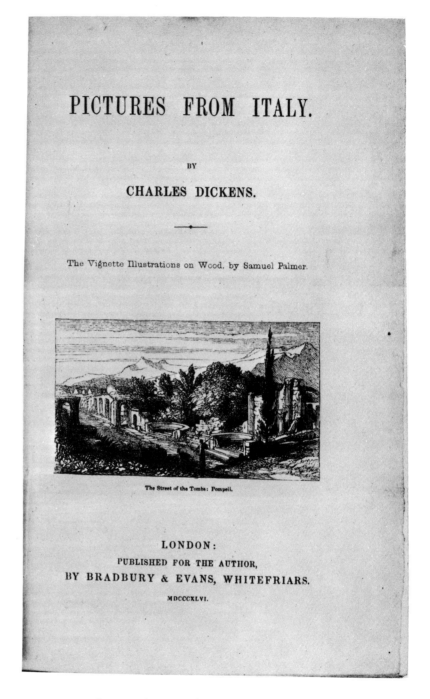

PICTURES FROM ITALY.

BY

CHARLES DICKENS.

The Vignette Illustrations on Wood, by Samuel Palmer.

The Street of the Tombs: Pompeii.

LONDON:
PUBLISHED FOR THE AUTHOR,
BY BRADBURY & EVANS, WHITEFRIARS.
MDCCCXLVI.

Pictures from Italy. London, Bradbury and Evans, 1846.

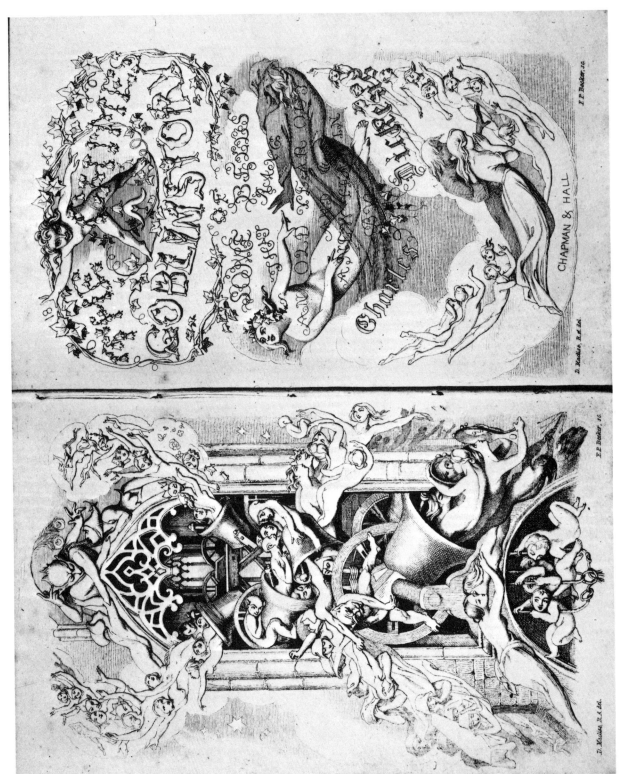

The Chimes: A Goblin Story of Some Bells that Rang an Old Year Out and a New Year In.
London, Chapman and Hall, 1845.

" 'It's a great thing to have my title, and see my way how to work the bells. Let them clash upon me now

So, May and Edward get up, amid great applause, to dance

alone ; and Bertha plays her liveliest tune.

Well! if you'll believe me, they have not been dancing

"Late in 1845 Dickens began the writing of his third Christmas Book, the title of which grew out of an idea to begin the publication of a weekly periodical which was to be called 'The Cricket,' with an added motto, 'A cheerful creature that chirrups on the Hearth.' The proposition was abandoned in favour of a more important venture, which resulted in the founding of *The Daily News*. Afterwards the idea of the periodical found fruition in the launching of *Household Words*."

(John C. Eckel, *The First Editions of the Writings of Charles Dickens*, London, 1913.)

It is a copy of the seventh edition that Dickens, as was his habit, marked up as his prompt copy to serve him during his public readings on the platform. The first reading of *The Cricket* was given on December 29, 1853, two days after the first reading of the *Carol*. It was another benefit reading for the new Midland Institute. Another heavily revised text, this copy was bound for Dickens for his library, and it bears his bookplate.

The Cricket on the Hearth. Seventh edition. London, Bradbury and Evans, 1846.

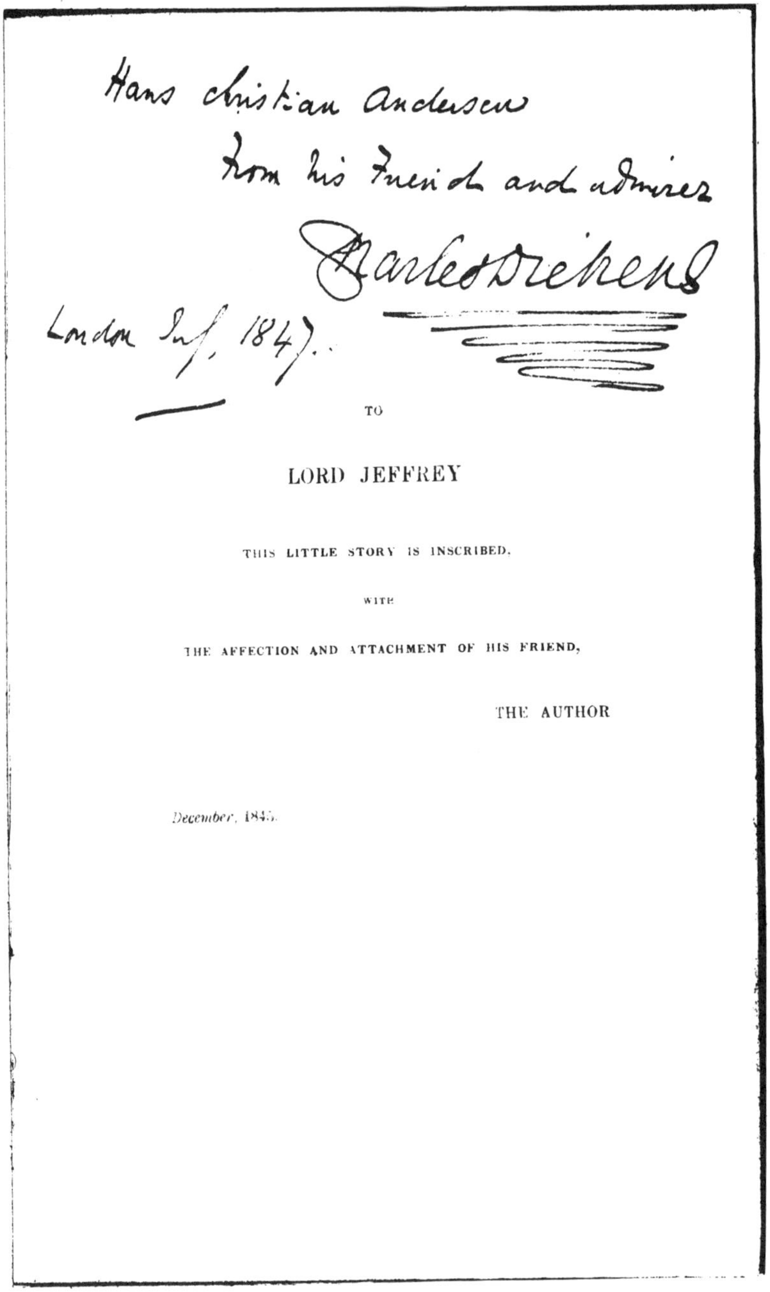

Hans christian Andersen
from his friend and admirer
Charles Dickens
London July 1847.

TO

LORD JEFFREY

THIS LITTLE STORY IS INSCRIBED,

WITH

THE AFFECTION AND ATTACHMENT OF HIS FRIEND,

THE AUTHOR

December, 1845.

The Cricket on the Hearth. Twenty-first edition.
London, Bradbury and Evans, 1846.

The story was immensely popular, doubling the circulation of both of its predecessors. Twenty-one editions were published during the first year of its appearance. In July, 1847, Hans Christian Andersen received from "his friend and admirer" an inscribed copy. They were good friends and in 1851 when Dickens moved to Tavistock House in Tavistock Square, the Danish visitor had a snug room looking out on the garden. In 1857 he stayed with the family at Gad's Hill, but he outstayed his welcome. When he left, Dickens stuck a card on his dressing-table mirror, reading: "Hans Christian Andersen slept in this room for five weeks which seemed to the family ages."

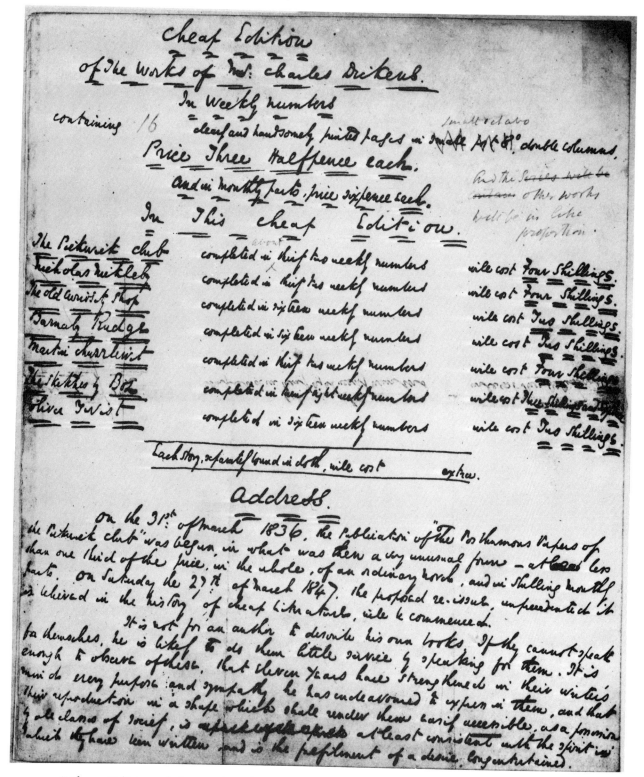

"Cheap Edition of the Works of Mr Charles Dickens . . . Address." Manuscript draft.

". . . by the middle of December [1846] he was able to dash over to London to settle the form for a new cheap edition of his books and help the Keeleys stage *The Battle of Life* at the Lyceum Theatre. The cheap edition was printed in double columns, without illustrations, in weekly numbers at three halfpence each, and dedicated 'to the English people, in whose approval, if the books be true in spirit, they will live, and out of whose memory, if they be false, they will very soon die.' "

(Edgar Johnson, *Charles Dickens.*)

109

"*The Battle of Life* was published with illustrations by Stanfield, Maclise, Leech, and Doyle, and dedicated to the author's English friends in Switzerland. It does not hold a place with its Christmas predecessors, having little originality in design or execution, and bearing traces of the fatigue with which it was produced."

(John Forster, *Forster's Life of Dickens.*
Abridged and revised by George Gissing.)

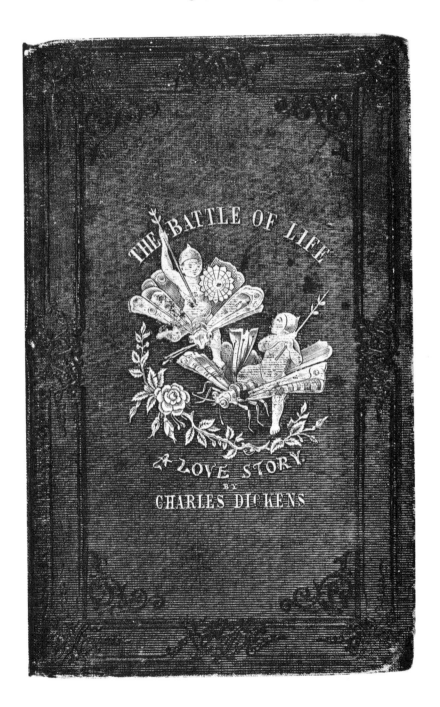

The Battle of Life. London, Bradbury & Evans, 1846.

Letter to Emile De la Rue, Paris, January 22, 1847.

48 Rue de Courcelles, Paris.
Twenty Second January 1847

My Dear De la Rue

Of course you think I am a forgetful vagabond. But I am not. A hundred occupations and distractions here combined to preventing writing to anyone — and a parcel designed for Madame De la Rue has entered into the conspiracy, and never came here from England. But Forster, who is here now, and returns home tomorrow week, will send me another parcel immediately on his arrival, — and before I dispatch it I will write you a long letter, containing all the news I can think of.

You will be glad, I know, to hear in the meanwhile that The Battle of Life has beaten all the other Christmas Books out of the field: and that Dombey is doing wonders. You run away at Railroad speed (and more than Railroad speed) in estimating its profits; but I will set you right in that long epistle I am going to perpetrate.

Give my love to Madame De la Rue, and tell her I have become an accomplished Frenchman. And entreat her never to suppose when I am tardy in my correspondence, that I am unmindful of my friends. It would be difficult to do me a greater injustice.

To William and all remembering friends — Consuls, Butlers, Gibbses, and the rest — give my regards. Expect a letter of such tremendous length as shall make your hair stand on end!

Ever Cordially Yours
Charles Dickens

Emile De la Rue was a Swiss banker who, with his pretty English wife, had met Dickens during his stay in Genoa. During their friendship over the years Dickens had a bizarre relationship with Madame whom he tried to help with mesmerism. This ultimately aroused the jealousy of Mrs. Dickens.

"*The Haunted Man* was published, with illustrations by Tenniel, Leech, Clarkson Stanfield, and Frank Stone, on December 19th, and sold eighteen thousand copies before evening of that day. Toward the end of the year a dramatic version by Mark Lemon was produced with considerable success at the Adelphi Theatre. Dickens gave some aid in the writing and rehearsal of the play, though his feelings about the dramatization of a novelist's works remained unaltered. 'But in the accursed state of the law on this subject,' he explained to his father-in-law George Hogarth, 'I have no power to prevent it; and therefore I think it is best to have at least one Theatre where it is done in a less Beastly manner than at others, and where I can impress *something* (however little) on the actors.' "

(Edgar Johnson, *Charles Dickens.*)

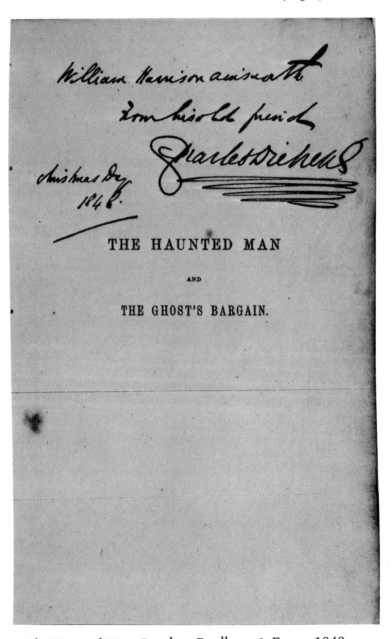

The Haunted Man. London, Bradbury & Evans, 1848.

This copy of the first edition was inscribed by Dickens to
William Harrison Ainsworth on Christmas Day, 1848.

After *The Haunted Man* Dickens no longer published separate Christmas books, but celebrated the occasion with special numbers of *Household Words*. When the first number of *All the Year Round* announced on May 28, 1859, that it also incorporated *Household Words*, the reading public was reassured of their Extra Christmas Numbers.

"...the triumph of the Christmas achievements in these days was Mrs. Lirriper. She took her place at once among people known to everybody; and all the world talked of Major Jemmy Jackman, and his friend the poor elderly lodging-house keeper of the Strand, with her miserable cares and rivalries and worries, as if they had both been as long in London and as well known as Norfolk-street itself."

(John Forster, *The Life of Charles Dickens.*)

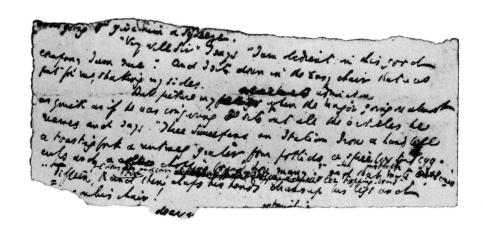

A portion of the manuscript of "Mrs. Lirriper's Lodgings,"
the Extra Christmas Number of *All the Year Round*,
Christmas, 1863.

rooms thereof, taking my evening cobbler, julep, sling, or cocktail. Again, I listened to my friend the General—whom I had known for five minutes, in the course of which period he had made me intimate for life with two Majors, who again had made me intimate for life with three Colonels, who again had made me brother to twenty-two civilians—again, I say, I listened to my friend the General, leisurely expounding the resources of the establishment, as to gentlemen's morning-room, sir; ladies' morning-room, sir; gentlemen's evening-room, sir; ladies' evening-room, sir; ladies' and gentlemen's evening re-uniting-room, sir; music-room, sir; reading room, sir; over four-hundred sleeping-rooms, sir; and the entire planned and finited within twelve calendar months from the first clearing off of the old incumbrances on the plot, at a cost of five hundred thousand dollars, sir. Again I found, as to my individual way of thinking, that the greater, the more gorgeous, and the more dollarous, the establishment was, the less desirable it was. Nevertheless, again I drank my cobbler, julep, sling, or cocktail, in all good-will, to my friend the General, and my friends the Majors, Colonels, and civilians, all; full-well knowing that whatever little motes my beamy eyes may have descried in theirs, they belong to a kind, generous, large-hearted, and great people.

I had been going on lately, at a quick pace, to keep my solitude out of my mind; but, here I broke down for good, and gave up the subject. What was I to do? What was to become of me? Into what extremity was I submissively to sink? Supposing that, like Baron Trenck, I looked out for a mouse or spider, and found one, and beguiled my imprisonment by training it? Even that might be dangerous with a view to the future. I might be so far gone when the road did come to be cut through the snow, that, on my way forth, I might burst into tears, and beseech, like the prisoner who was released in his old age from the Bastille, to be taken back again to the five windows, the ten curtains, and the sinuous drapery.

A desperate idea came into my head. Under any other circumstances I should have rejected it; but, in the strait at which I was, I held it fast. Could I so far overcome the inherent bashfulness which withheld me from the landlord's table and the company I might find there, as to make acquaintance, under various pretences, with some of the inmates of the house, singly—with the object of getting from each, either a whole autobiography, or a passage or experience in one, with which I could cheat the tardy time: first of all by seeking out, then by listening to, then by remembering and writing down? Could I, I asked myself, so far overcome my retiring nature as to do this? I could. I would. I did.

The results of this conception I proceed to give, in the exact order in which I attained them. I began my plan of operations at once, and, by slow approaches and after overcoming many obstacles (all of my own making, I believe), reached the story of:

THE OSTLER.

I FIND an old man, fast asleep, in one of the stalls of the stable. It is mid-day, and rather a strange time for an ostler to devote to sleep. Something curious, too, about the man's face. A withered woe-begone face. The eyebrows painfully contracted; the mouth fast set, and drawn down at the corners; the hollow cheeks sadly, and, as I cannot help fancying, prematurely wrinkled; the scanty, grizzled hair, telling weakly its own tale of some past sorrow or suffering. How fast he draws his breath, too, for a man asleep! He is talking in his sleep.

"Wake up!" I hear him say, in a quick whisper through his fast-clenched teeth. "Wake up there! Murder! O Lord help me! Lord help me, alone in this place!"

He stops, and sighs again—moves one lean arm slowly, till it rests over his throat—shudders a little, and turns on his straw—the arm leaves his throat—the hand stretches itself out, and clutches at the side towards which he has turned, as if he fancies himself to be grasping at the edge of something. Is he waking? No—there is the whisper again; he is still talking in his sleep.

"Light grey eyes," he says now, "and a droop in the left eyelid. Yes! yes!—flaxen hair with a gold-yellow streak in it—all right, mother—fair, white arms with a down on them—little lady's hand, with a reddish look under the finger-nails—and the knife—always the cursed knife—first on one side, then on the other. Aha! you she-devil, where's the knife? Never mind, mother—too late now. I've promised to marry, and marry I must. Murder! wake up there! for God's sake, wake up!"

At the last words his voice rises, and he grows so restless on a sudden, that I draw back quietly to the door. I see him shudder on the straw—his withered face grows distorted—he throws up both his hands with a quick, hysterical gasp; they strike against the bottom of the manger under which he lies; the blow awakens him; I have just time to slip through the door, before his eyes are fairly open and his senses are his own again.

What I have seen and heard has so startled and shocked me, that I feel my heart beating fast, as I softly and quickly retrace my steps across the inn-yard. The discomposure that is going on within me, apparently shows itself in my face; for, as I get back to the covered way leading to the Inn stairs, the landlord, who is just coming out of the house to ring some bell in the yard, stops astonished, and asks what is the matter with me? I tell him what I have just seen.

call up the Boots, and ask him to take a chair along with us — and something of a 'liquid form — and talk over it?

Household Words. The Extra Christmas Number, 1855.

This page shows how copies were corrected by Dickens and sent to the United States for American editors.

"Wal'r, my boy," replied the Captain, "in the Proverbs of Solomon you will find the following words, 'May we never want a friend in need, nor a bottle to give him!' When found, make a note of."

(*Dombey and Son*, Chapter XV.)

Letter to Emile De la Rue, Lausanne, October 12, 1846.

Rosemont, Lausanne
Monday Twelfth October 1846.

My Dear De la Rue

I have been at Geneva (left there immediately before the Revolution) and then found Serjeant Talfourd waiting for me here, whom I saw away to Basle. I am only just now in the receipt of your letter, and hasten to answer it, however briefly.

I think the best and plainest course will be for Madame to say nothing about us in her letter to Mrs Thompson — taking anything for granted, and mentioning, as it were incidentally, that you are just then writing to me. It seems a course that will suit anything and save a whole world of chances.

Dombey and Son is a most immense success. There is every present reason to suppose that it will beat all the other books. I am just going to sit down to the last part of the Christmas Volume. My work has been very severe of late.

I hope to be in Paris about the middle of next month; and from thence I will somehow send you my aforesaid books, please God. Give my best love to Madame. I came back rather drearily from Vevay that night. We had a happy day, and will have many more please Heaven, somewhere or other.

In great haste
Ever affectionately Yours
CD

Remember me to Brown. I dined with Lady Walpole and Lady Pellen at Geneva the other day.

Dickens began work on *Dombey* in June, 1846, in Lausanne, Switzerland, where he and the family stayed until November, 1846. Three months of the new year were spent in Paris, from where Dickens returned to England in February, 1847.

The central idea of the new story was that it "should do with Pride what its predecessor [*Martin Chuzzlewit*] had done with Selfishness." An outstanding theme is the attack on the importance attached to money. The success of *Dombey*, much greater than that of *Martin Chuzzlewit*, marked a turning point in Dickens's life. He had recovered the control of half his copyrights, and the continuing sale of earlier books combined with the splendid profits of *Dombey* made him prosperous beyond all further worry.

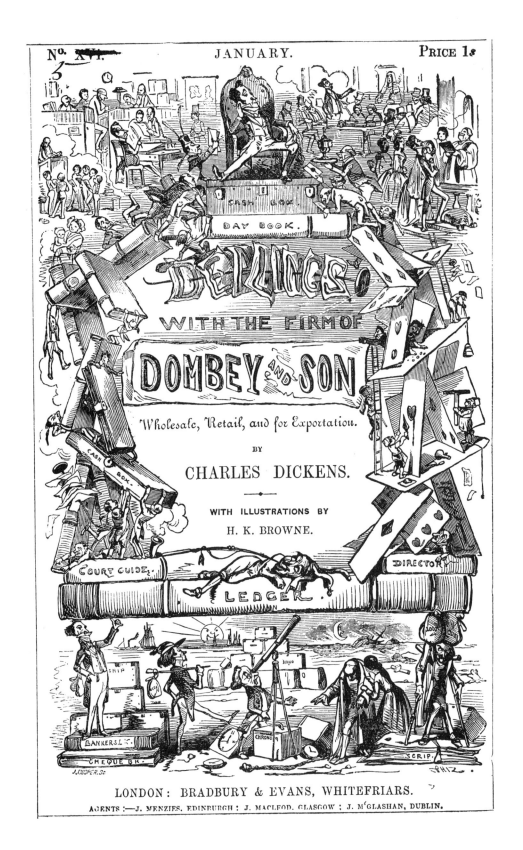

Dealings with the Firm of Dombey and Son, Wholesale, Retail and for Exportation. No. 1, October [1846]-No. 19-20, April [1848]. London, Bradbury & Evans. No. 5 is illustrated here.

Letter to William Makepeace Thackeray, [London] March 30, 1848.

Devonshire Terrace
Thirteenth March 1848.

My Dear Thackeray.
   I propose holding a solemn dinner here, on Tuesday the 11th of April, to celebrate the conclusion of a certain immortal book. Hour, halfpast six. It couldn't be done without you. Therefore, book it cher citoyen! —

Ever Faithfully Yours
Charles Dickens

Letter to Hablôt K. Browne, [London] June 13, 1848.

Devonshire Terrace
Thirteenth June 1848

My Dear Browne.
   A thousand thanks for the Dombey sketches, which I shall preserve and transmit as heirlooms.
   This afternoon, or Thursday, I shall be near the whereabout of the boy in the flannel gown, and will pay him an affectionate visit. But I warn you now and beforehand (and this is final you'll observe) that you are not a going to back out of the pigmental finishing of said boy, for if ever I had a boy of my own, that boy is

MINE!

and, as the Demon says at the Surrey

I CLAIM MY VICTIM.
HA! HA! HA!

at which you will imagine me going down a sulphurous trap, with the boy in my grasp — and you will please not to imagine him merely, in my grasp, but to hand him over.
   For which this is your warrant and requirement.

(signed)
Charles Dickens

Witness   ✕
William Topping
    his
    Groom

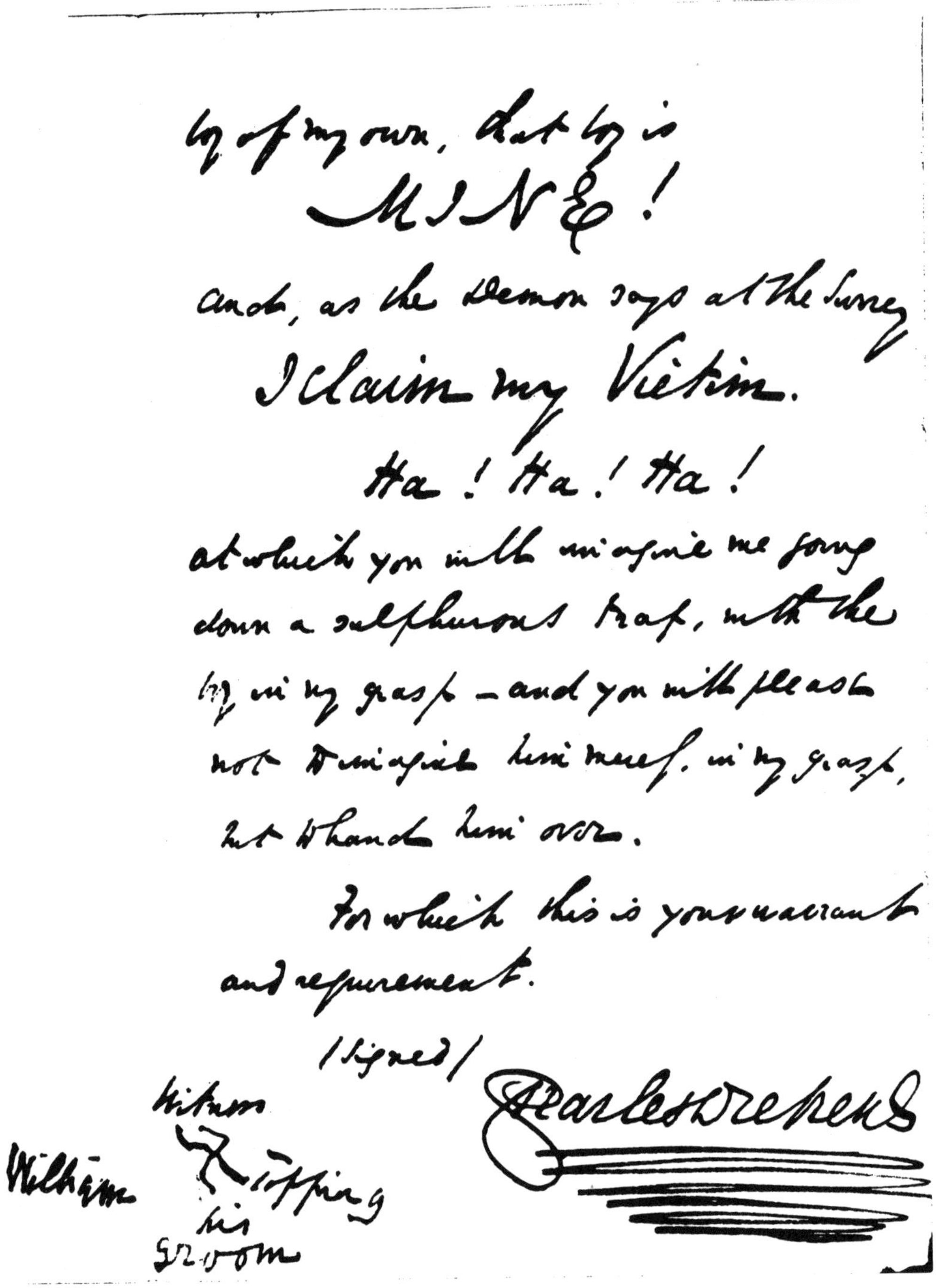

y of my own, that y is

MINE!

And, as the Demon says at the Surrey

I claim my Victim.

Ha! Ha! Ha!

at which you will imagine me going
down a sulphurous trap, with the
y in my grasp — and you will please
not to imagine him meanwhile, in my grasp,
but to hand him over.

For which this is your warrant
and requirement.

[Signed]

Witness
William Ripping
his
Groom

Charles Dickens

Conclusion of letter to Hablôt K. Browne, [London] June 13, 1848.

Dealings with the Firm of Dombey and Son, Wholesale, Retail, and for Exportation. London, Bradbury & Evans, 1848.

Original drawing by Hablôt K. Browne, "Captain Cuttle consoles his friend."

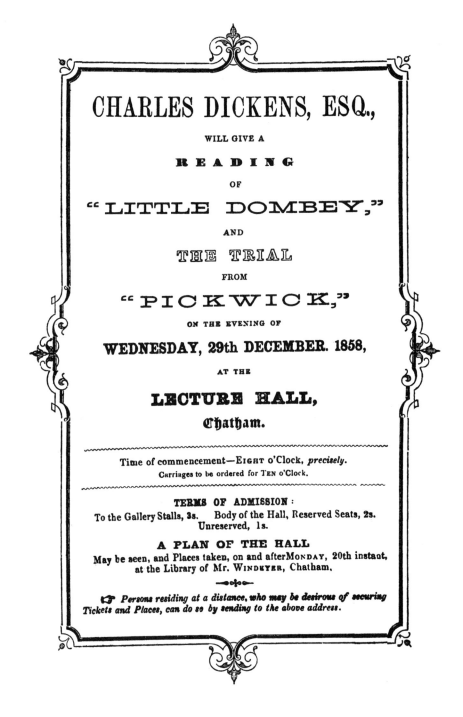

Announcement for Reading by Dickens on December 29, 1858, at the Lecture Hall, Chatham.

This broadside is inserted in the presentation copy Dickens inscribed to his companion in Lausanne, William Haldimand, a former member of Parliament, who became the godfather of Dickens's seventh child, born on April 18, 1847, christened Sydney Smith Haldimand Dickens.

"We had an amazing scene of weeping and cheering, at St. Martin's Hall last night. I read the Life and Death of Little Dombey: and I certainly never saw a crowd so resolved into one creature before, or so stirred by anything," wrote Dickens to John Forster. The abbreviated story of Paul Dombey, which, in the original publication, ended in Part 5 with his death, reduced the public to tears. Only the death of Little Nell elicited comparable emotion. Dickens wrote to Miss Burdett-Coutts from Paris on January 18, 1847: "...Paul is dead. He died on Friday night about 10 o'clock, and as I had no hope of getting to sleep afterwards, I went out, and walked about Paris until breakfast time next morning...."

Harry Burnett, the little crippled boy of Dickens's eldest sister Fanny Burnett, who died soon after his mother in 1848. He is supposed to be the original of Paul Dombey and Tiny Tim.

This photograph was once the property of Elizabeth Dickens, mother of Charles Dickens.

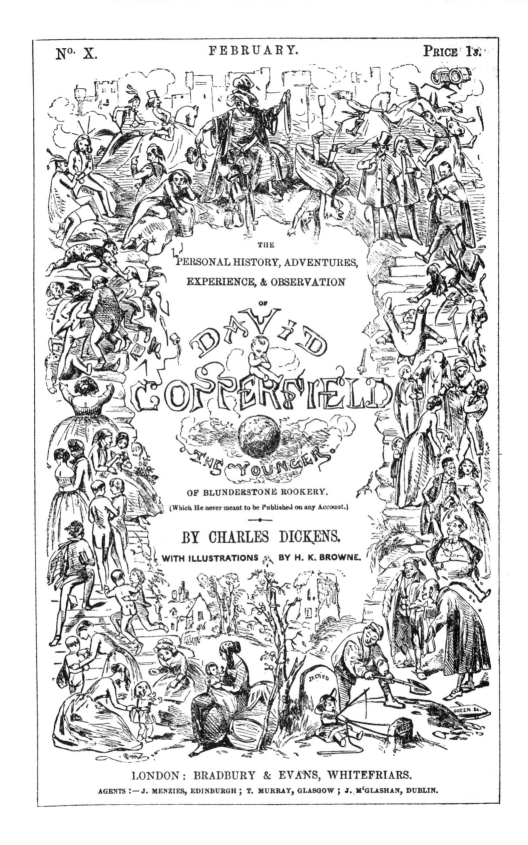

The Personal History, Adventures, Experience, & Observation of David Copperfield the Younger. No. 1, May [1849]-No. 19-20, November [1850]. London, Bradbury & Evans.

No. 10 is illustrated here.

Several months before *David Copperfield* was begun Dickens showed John Forster a sketch of his own early life and hardships. Towards 1848 he was working out ideas for a new story, which he was writing experimentally as an autobiography of the hero. In this scheme he saw the usefulness of his own autobiographical narrative would have for the novel. The story became a mixture of Dickens's personal experience and imagination.

One copy of the first edition in book form (1850) was inscribed by Dickens to William Henry Wills, formerly his secretary on the *Daily News* and after March 30, 1850, the assistant editor of Dickens's new venture, *Household Words*. Another decade later, when Dickens started his weekly journal, *All the Year Round*, Wills became part owner.

"I was thinking of all that had been said. My mind was still running on some of the expressions used. 'There can be no disparity in marriage like unsuitability of mind and purpose.' 'The first mistaken impulse of an undisciplined heart.' 'My love was founded on a rock.' But we are at home; and the trodden leaves were lying underfoot, and the autumn wind was blowing."

(*David Copperfield*, Chapter XLV.)

"Of all my books, I like this the best. It will be easily believed that I am a fond parent to every child of my fancy, and that no one can ever love that family as dearly as I love them. But, like many fond parents, I have in my heart of hearts a favourite child. And his name is DAVID COPPERFIELD."

(*David Copperfield*, Preface to the Charles Dickens edition, 1869.)

"I was in Switzerland. I had come out of Italy, over one of the great passes of the Alps, and had since wandered with a guide among the byways of the mountains. If those awful solitudes had spoken to my heart, I did not know it. I had found sublimity and wonder in the dread heights and precipices, in the roaring torrents, and the wastes of ice and snow, but, as yet, they had taught me nothing else."

(*David Copperfield*, Chapter LVIII.)

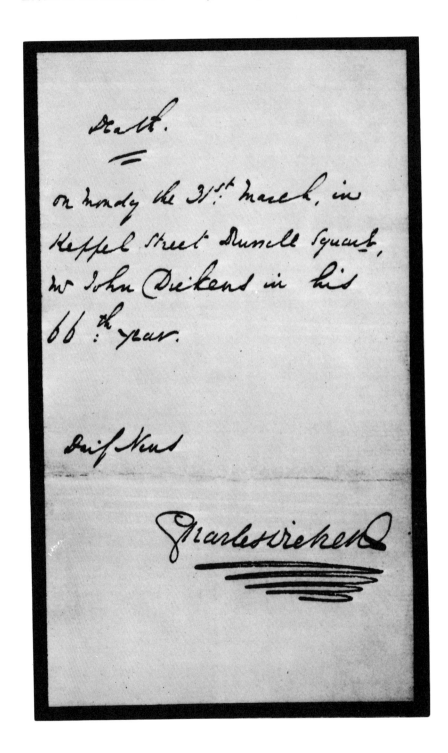

Dickens founded the *Daily News* in 1846 and appointed his father to be in charge of the reporting staff.

Letter to Emile De la Rue, London, April 25, 1851.

Devonshire Terrace, London
Twenty Fifth April, 1851.

My Dear De la Rue.

I should have written to you long ago; but many distractions (among them the sickness and death of my father, and the sudden death of our baby-daughter — Dora, in remembrance of Copperfield) have shaken me from my desk for a little while.

A thousand thanks for your kindness to our old cook, who brought with her a most earnest and pathetic remembrance of it, I assure you. She is now happily married and staying with her sister. We lost no time in getting it done as lawfully as priests, Protestant and Roman, could do it. They have been married in both churches, and are (I suppose) doubly blessed. We are exceedingly thankful to you and Madame De la Rue for your care of her. I cannot tell you how much so.

London is filling to that preposterous extent ahead, that we are going down to the Sea-side, to remain there all the Season. Of course you and Madame De la Rue mean to come to the Exhibition, and of course you'll let me know of your whereabout. (My address will be Broadstairs, Kent). I am at present up to the throat in work. You may have seen in the papers that Bulwer, I, and some others, have a design for the establishment of a certain "Guild of Literature and Art." To set it going, he has written a new comedy, which is to be played at The Duke of Devonshire's, under my management, before The Queen. All day long, and half the night sometimes, we are roaring away at this (the undersigned amidst a mob of carpenters, upholsterers, theatrical supernumeraries, tailors, wig-makers, and Heaven knows what else) until we can hardly stagger home. It comes out on the 16th and I shall have no peace until that night is over.

My love to my dear old Patient. But for this design, I should have seen you both this Spring; for I had made up my mind to run over to Genoa and Venice. I live in hope. The Examiner, I fear, is getting fearfully irregular! It goes to Charley at Eton, and never comes back — and he ought to post it, and never does. I enclose a piece of my heart in this hasty note, and beg you to be careful of it as you take it in your pocket up those stairs, and across those landings, and past all those busts, and up that upper staircase, and so come to the bell-pull, which Michele (or some one else) answers, and so lets you into the room where the tea used to be on hot nights. My God, how well I remember it all! I seem to look down out of the high windows, out of breath, now I have got up there!

Ever Faithfully Yours My Dear De la Rue
Charles Dickens

Dora Annie Dickens was born on August 16, 1850, and died on April 14, 1851. Kate Dickens, overwhelmed with grief, wanted to go away to Broadstairs; the lease at Devonshire Terrace was to expire in September.

1851 was the year of the Great Exhibition which attracted large crowds to London.

Sir Edward Bulwer-Lytton's Not So Bad as We Seem was played to the Queen at Devonshire House on May 16th and was then taken on a provincial tour with great success.

Throughout the rest of his life, Dickens gave the Guild of Literature and Art his faithful service, in the capacity of the Chairman.

Hablôt K. Browne ("Phiz"). "The friendly waiter
and I." *David Copperfield*, Chapter IV. Original
pen and wash drawing on tissue paper.

Hablôt K. Browne ("Phiz"). "My child-wife's old companion." *David Copperfield*, Chapter LI. Original pen and wash drawing on tissue paper.

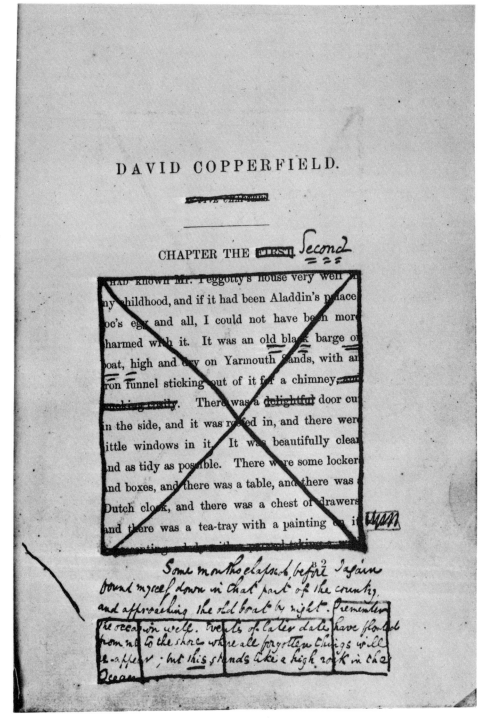

David Copperfield. A Reading. [London] Privately printed [n.d.].

The first public reading of *David Copperfield* took place in Norwich on October 28, 1861. The copy that served Dickens as his prompt copy and in which he perfected the text was again bound for him and placed in his library.

Although at Norwich the reading was not a success, in Edinburgh at the beginning of December, 1861, Dickens could write that *Copperfield* was "without precedent in the reading chronicles. Four rounds when I went in — laughing and crying and thundering all the time — a great burst of cheering at last."

Bleak House. No. 1, March [1852]-No. 19-20, September [1853].
London, Bradbury & Evans. No. 3 is illustrated here.

At the end of November, 1851, almost as soon as the family settled in Tavistock House, Dickens began work on what was to become an attack on the Court of Chancery. The date of the first number, in March, 1852, coincided with that of the birth of the youngest child who, after his godfather, was named Edward Bulwer Lytton Dickens.

"It is a melancholy truth that even great men have their poor relations."

(*Bleak House*, Chapter XXVIII.)

"The portraiture of two of the prominent characters in *Bleak House* was undoubtedly inspired by living personages. The Novelist's friend, Walter Savage Landor, is admitted to be the original of Lawrence Boythorne. Thomas Carlyle called Landor the 'unsubduable Roman,' and the late Mrs. Lynn Linton, who knew him intimately, records that he was irascible and obstinate ... Although by no means an unpleasing portrait, he apparently did not relish the liberty which Dickens had taken with his personality ... With regard to the second portrait, that of Harold Skimpole, in whom are embodied the more pronounced idiosyncrasies of Leigh Hunt, the consequences were more lamentable, inasmuch as grave offence was unintentionally given to the author of 'Rimini ...' "

(Frederic G. Kitton, *Charles Dickens*.)

Bleak House. London, Bradbury and Evans, 1853.

The work was issued in book form almost simultaneously with the last number of the serial publication and was dedicated "as a remembrance of our friendly union," to the members of the Guild of Literature and Art. In token of appreciation to a member, Peter Cunningham, Dickens inscribed a presentation copy on October 3, 1853. Cunningham was famous for his *Handbook of London*, 1849, and was a frequent performer in Dickens's amateur theatricals.

"England has been in a dreadful state for some weeks. Lord Coodle would go out, and Sir Thomas Doodle wouldn't come in, and there being nobody in Great Britain (to speak of) except Coodle and Doodle, there has been no Government."

(*Bleak House*, Chapter XL.)

"I only ask to be free. The butterflies are free. Mankind will surely not deny to Harold Skimpole what it concedes to the butterflies!"

(*Bleak House*, Chapter VI.)

Hablôt K. Browne ("Phiz"). "Attorney and Client, fortitude and impatience." *Bleak House*, Chapter XXXIX. Original pencil drawing.

"But the struggle to forge the gigantic attainment of *Bleak House* into its huge unit had momentarily exhausted Dickens's powers. He must have rest before he undertook another work of fiction. And so, after his heavy spell of labor, he made ready now in the autumn of 1853 to set out on a two-month holiday in Switzerland and Italy that he had been planning from the preceding January to take with Augustus Egg and Wilkie Collins.

Since Egg had induced Collins to play the valet in *Not So Bad as We Seem*, a genial association had developed between Dickens and the younger writer."

(Edgar Johnson, Charles Dickens.)

Letter to Georgina Hogarth, Venice, November 25, 1853.

Venice, Friday Twenty Fifth November 1853

My Dearest Georgy,

I received your capital letter just now on sending to the Post office, and read it with the greatest pleasure. I think you will not find that I shall neglect anything you "leave" for me to do and see when I come home!

Kate's letter, written and posted at Bonchurch at the same time, I received with yours. But the missing letter addressed to Florence has not yet come to hand. Tell her with my best love that I therefore defer writing to <u>her</u>, until tomorrow, <u>in the hope that I may then be able to say I have received it.</u> I left instructions at the Hotel that it should be applied for again after the next post came in, and forwarded here. It could hardly have been here this morning, as we left before the Courier and travelled as fast.

We found an English carriage from Padua at Florence, and hired it to bring it back again. We travelled post with four horses all the way (from Padua to this place there is a railroad) and travelled all night. We left Florence at halfpast 6 in the morning, and got to Padua at eleven next day — yesterday. The cold at night was most intense. I don't think I have ever felt it colder. But our carriage was very comfortable, and we had some wine and some rum to keep us warm. We came by Bologna (where we had tea) and Ferrara. You may imagine the delays in the night when I tell you that each of our passports, after receiving <u>6 vises</u> at Florence, received, in the course of the one night, <u>Nine more</u>, everyone of which was written and sealed; somebody being slowly knocked out of bed to do it every time! It really was excruciating.

Landor had sent me a letter to his son, and on the day before we left Florence I thought I would go out to Fiesole and leave it. So I got a little onehorse open carriage and drove off alone. We were within half a mile of the Villa Landora and were driving down a very narrow lane, like one of those at Albaro, when I saw an elderly lady coming towards us, very well dressed in silk of the Queen's blue, and walking freshly and briskly against the wind at a good round pace. It was a bright, cloudless, very cold day; and I thought she walked with great spirit, as if she enjoyed it. I also thought (perhaps that was having him in my mind) that her ruddy face was shaped like Landor's. All of a sudden the coachman pulls up, and looks enquiringly at me. "What's the matter?" says I. "Ecco la Signora Landora!" says he. "For the love of Heaven, don't stop!" says I. "<u>I</u> don't know her — I am only going to the house to leave a letter — Go on!" Meanwhile she (still coming on) looked at me, and I looked at her, and we were both a good deal confused, and so went our several ways. Altogether, I think it was as disconcerting a meeting as I ever took part in, and as odd a one. Under any other circumstances I should have introduced myself, but the separation made the circumstances so peculiar that I "didn't like."

The Plornishghenter is evidently the greatest, noblest, finest, cleverest, brightest, and most brilliant of boys. Your account of him is most delightful, and I hope to find another letter from you somewhere on the road, making me informed of his demeanour on your return. On which occasion, as on every other, I have no doubt he will have distinguished himself as an irresistibly attracting, captivating May-Roon-Ti-Goon-Ter. Give him a good many kisses for me, I quite agree with Syd as to his ideas of paying attention to the old gentleman. H. not bad, but deficient in originality. The usual deficiency of an inferior intellect with so great a model before him. I am very curious to see whether the Plorn remembers me on my reappearance.

A very good thing in two letters received from Wills and Forster at Rome. Forster tells me on the one hand how he has an account to give me of Wills and Miss Martineau together which will entertain me for evermore; and Wills writes that Forster with Miss Martineau was grand beyond description. Each so gloriously innocent of what the other writes.

I meant to have gone to work this morning and to have tried a second little story for the Xmas N° of Household Words, but my letters have (most pleasantly) put me out, and I defer all such wise efforts until tomorrow. Egg and Collins are out in a Gondola with a Servitore di Piazza; where, I have no doubt, Collins, unchecked by inattention and reveries on the part of the Inimitable, will deliver an entire course of Lectures on Art. He gave us by the by in a carriage one day, a full account of his first love adventure. It was at Rome it seemed and proceeded, if I may be allowed the expression, to the utmost extremities — he came out quite a pagan Jupiter in the business. Egg and I made a calculation afterwards, and found that at this precocious passage in his history, he was twelve years and some odd months old.

You will find this but a stupid letter, but I really have no news. We go to the Opera, wherever there is one, see sights, eat and drink, sleep in a natural manner two or three nights, and move on again. Eduard was a little crushed at Padua yesterday. He had been extraordinarily cold all night in the rumble, and had got out our clothes to dress, and I think must have been projecting a five or six hours sleep, when I announced that he was to come on here in an hour and a half to get the rooms and order dinner. He fell into a sudden despondency of the profoundest kind, but was quite restored when we arrived here between 8 and 9. We found him waiting at the Custom House with a gondola, in his usual brisk condition.

It is extraordinary how few English we see. With the exception of a gentlemanly young fellow (in a consumption I am afraid) married to the tiniest little girl in a brown straw hat, and travelling with his sister and her sister — and a consumptive single lady travelling with a maid and a Scotch Terrier christened Trotty Veck — we have scarcely seen any, and have certainly spoken to none, since we left Switzerland. These were aboard the Valetta, where the Captain and I indulged in all manner of insane suppositions concerning the straw hat — The Little Matron we called her; by which name she soon became known all over the ship. The day we entered Rome, and the moment we entered it, there was the Little Matron, alone with antiquity — and Murray — on the wall. The very first church I entered, there was the Little Matron. On the last afternoon, when I went alone to St Peters, there was the Little Matron and her party. The best of it is, that I was extremely intimate with them, invited them to Tavistock House when they come home in the Spring, and have not the faintest idea of their name.

There was no table d'hote at Rome, or at Florence; but there is one here and we dine at it to day, so perhaps we may stumble upon somebody. I have heard from Charley this morning who appoints (wisely) Paris as our place of meeting. I had a letter from Coote at Florence, informing me that his volume of "Household Songs" was ready, and requesting permission to dedicate it to me. Which of course I gave.

I am beginning to think of the Birmingham readings. I suppose you won't object to be taken to hear them? This is the last place at which we shall make a stay of more than one day. We shall stay at Parma one, and at Turin one (supposing De la Rue to have been suc-

cessful in taking places with the Courier into France for the day on which we want them; he was to write to bankers at Turin to do it) and then we shall come hard and fast home. I feel almost there already, and shall be delighted to close the pleasant trip and get back to my own *Piccola Camera* — if, being English, you understand what <u>that</u> is!

I am afraid you must have been fishing for a compliment when you talk about the postage of your letters, so I shall punish you by saying that indeed it does come heavy and that I would propose, if you see no objection, to make your mind easy on that score by stopping it out of your quarter. — Due I suppose by the by?

I cannot remember what Egg (to whom I will give your message when he comes back presently) called a Bird yesterday, in his second or third endeavour to explode a substantive on a waiter. But it was something compounded of English and French with an Italian termination — something like *Birdoisella*. I never in my life saw anyone naturally so slow to learn. He speaks of it himself as being something quite remarkable. He understands much more than you would suppose of what is said, but it is such a painful effort to him to acquire anything, although I have really taken pains to explain it with the greatest clearness and patience, that I doubt if he understands now in the least, about the Verb "To be" being conjugated with itself instead of with the Verb "To have". Collins perpetually breaks into French (though sagacious in the last degree about Italy, Italian, and the Italians), and takes that tongue under his particular protection. He is much troubled with a "tightness" in his inside, and is always reporting on its condition to us.

My best loves and kisses to Mamey, Katey, Sydney, Harry, and the noble Plorn. Last, not least, to yourself — and many of them. I will not wait over tomorrow, tell Kate, for her letter; but will write then, whether or no.

Ever My Dearest Georgy
most affectionately Yours
CD

P.S.
I have thought a good deal about Christiana, whom you mention. Her excitability and restlessness are a positive disease. — In defending her painting to me against the charges of Mrs Brown, she said — so fast, that she seemed to leave out all small words — "assure you Mr Dickens — shall see my pictures yet — in Exhibition in London Royal Academy. — Play great deal better since painted than ever did — positively great deal better. Painting's poetry and music's poetry, and poetry breaking out of a person in one, breaks out in the other — naturally — must be so!"

Gibbs shewed me a letter he had received a few weeks before from Thompson; introducing it in a speech half an hour long, of which I understood nothing but that the desire of his life — and one thing and another, you understand — (there he put his finger against the side of his nose) was to live in peace; and that if you took him as you found him, well and good; and that if you didn't — bene — siamo due! The letter referred to some "misunderstanding", arising out of Thompson's son in law having made observations to Madame Somebody, on the subject of his nose: implying in a general way that it was long enough for Mrs Thompson to lead him by it — which she did. It was a prodigious letter, of four close sides of paper. Gibbs had endorsed it outside, in a neat round business hand.

"Twaddle! Twaddle!! Twaddle!!!"

This had evidently relieved his mind immensely.

"Plorn," otherwise Edward Bulwer Lytton Dickens, for long his father's favorite child, showed no intellectual talents as he developed.

"H." otherwise "Harry," otherwise Sir Henry Fielding Dickens, proved himself later as barrister and author.

The T. J. Thompsons, old friends of Dickens, were at that time in Nervi. Mrs. Thompson, Christiana Weller, was once described by Dickens as an "ethereal creature."

"The work that next engaged the Novelist's attention was 'Hard Times, for these Times,' which he prepared as a serial in *Household Words*, where it appeared from 1st April to 12th August 1854. As explained to Charles Knight, his satire was directed against those 'who see figures and averages, and nothing else — the representatives of the wickedest and most enormous vice of this time — the men who, through long years to come, will do more to damage the real useful truths of political economy than I could do (if I tried) in my whole life . . .' "

(Frederic G. Kitton, *Charles Dickens*.)

Letter to Bradbury and Evans, [London] March 7, 1854.

Tavistock House
Tuesday Seventh March 1854

My Dear B and E.
Throughout Hard Times, will you arrange when you get the corrected revises back from me (I now send those of the two first parts) to have them *pulled, for my reference copy at work, a proof folded in any easy form for reference that may not give much trouble to your people. I want to avoid the botheration, both of the long slips, and of having to cut my working copy out of the N^{os} week by week.*
Faithfully Yours always
CD

"Now, what I want is, Facts. . . . Facts alone are wanted in life."

(*Hard Times*, Book I, Chapter I.)

No. IV. MARCH. PRICE 1s.

LITTLE DORRIT

BY

CHARLES DICKENS.

WITH

ILLUSTRATIONS BY H. K. BROWNE.

LONDON: BRADBURY & EVANS, BOUVERIE STREET.
AGENTS: J. MENZIES, EDINBURGH; MURRAY AND SON, GLASGOW; J. M'GLASHAN, DUBLIN.

The Author reserves the right of Translation.

Little Dorrit. No. 1, December [1855]-No. 19-20, June [1857]. London, Bradbury & Evans. No. 4 is illustrated here.

From October, 1855, until May, 1856, Dickens lived in Paris, paying occasional visits to England. The story of *Little Dorrit* reflects the restlessness of the times — the Crimean war had just ended — and the restlessness of the author, who, "prowling wretchedly about the rooms on the Champs Elysées," described himself as "a Monster to my family, a dread phenomenon to myself." The story turned into a scathing attack on officialdom and evoked all the old memories of the Marshalsea Prison. The personal unhappiness was finally thought to be resolved in a separation by Dickens from his wife of twenty-two years. By the summer of 1858 his personal friends and the literary circle in London were divided in their loyalties. The public was told through the columns of *Household Words* on June 12, 1858, that "some domestic trouble of mine, of long-standing," had "lately been brought to an arrangement."

Hablôt K. Browne ("Phiz"). "Little Dorrit." Original pencil drawing for the engraved title page.

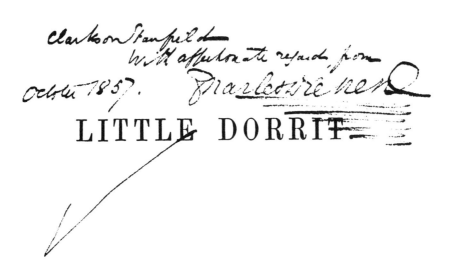

LITTLE DORRIT

BY

CHARLES DICKENS.

WITH ILLUSTRATIONS BY H. K. BROWNE.

LONDON:

BRADBURY AND EVANS, 11, BOUVERIE STREET.

1857.

Little Dorrit. London, Bradbury and Evans, 1857.

The new novel was dedicated to Dickens's old artist friend, Clarkson Stanfield. The dedication copy, with an inscription and an accompanying letter, was sent to the recipient on October 16, 1857.

"Whatever was required to be done, the Circumlocution Office was beforehand with all the public with all the departments in the art of perceiving – HOW NOT TO DO IT."

(*Little Dorrit*, Book I, Chapter X.)

Letter to Clarkson Stanfield, Office of *Household Words*, London, October 16, 1857.

No 16, Wellington Street North Strand
Friday Sixteenth October 1857

My Dear Stanny

I am extremely sorry to hear that you have been ill and confined to the house. I have been far away, and very busy, and much distressed by some anxieties, or I should have heard of you sooner.

Tomorrow forenoon I hope to be able to come out to Hampstead and shake you by the hand. In the meantime here is an old little friend in a new frock, who has been long due, and who begs to be tenderly taken in.

Ever affectionately
Charles Dickens

Little Dorrit. London, Chapman and Hall [n.d.].
Detail from title page.

"Little Dorrit," said Bernard Shaw, "is a more seditious book than *Das Kapital.* All over Europe men and women are in prison for pamphlets and speeches which are to *Little Dorrit* as red pepper to dynamite."

When in 1929 he sent an inscribed copy of the story to the American impresario, Merle Armitage, Bernard Shaw wrote on the fly-leaf the following: ". . . It is in some respects Dickens's greatest book, following the change to complete seriousness which was marked by his Hard Times. . . . My old friend and political colleague Sidney Webb, now Lord Passfield, also had his mind formed in youth by another copy of the Phiz Little Dorrit which his parents left lying about."

Letter to his brother, Alfred Lamert Dickens, London, October 11, 1856.

Tavistock House, London
Saturday Eleventh October 1856

My Dear Alfred.

I don't know whether you would care to be in a new play by Collins (which I am going to get up for Twelfth Night) for the mere sake of being in the social amusement of the Thing, or whether you are so certain of your movements as to be safely available if you do care.

But it has come into my head in casting about for somebody of your build and look, for a certain Sea-Captain who has some six lines to speak, and a little that is picturesque and requires care, to do in action, that you might like to be in the interest of the getting-up. Therefore I mention it to you first of all. Do exactly as you feel inclined, for I shall have no difficulty in finding this Captain's representative anyhow.

I will tell you all about it whenever you like. The preparations are tremendous, and the arrangements will be of stupefying grandeur.

With love to Helen and all the children, in which all here join.

Ever affectionately
CD

"*The Frozen Deep* had its first night on January 6, 1857, Charley's twentieth birthday, and there were three repeat performances, on the 8th, 12th, and 14th. Close to a hundred people crowded the little schoolroom theater each evening, although the ladies' crinolines made it a tight squeeze."

(Edgar Johnson, *Charles Dickens.*)

IN REMEMBRANCE OF THE LATE MR. DOUGLAS JERROLD.
LAST REPRESENTATION.

GALLERY OF ILLUSTRATION,
REGENT STREET.

UNDER THE MANAGEMENT OF MR. CHARLES DICKENS.

On Saturday evening, August 8th, 1857, AT 8 O'CLOCK EXACTLY, *will be presented*
FOR THE LAST TIME,
AN ENTIRELY NEW
ROMANTIC DRAMA, IN THREE ACTS, BY MR. WILKIE COLLINS,
CALLED

THE FROZEN DEEP.

PERFORMED BY THE AMATEUR COMPANY OF LADIES AND GENTLEMEN WHO
ORIGINALLY REPRESENTED IT, IN PRIVATE.

THE OVERTURE COMPOSED EXPRESSLY FOR THIS PIECE BY MR. FRANCESCO BERGER.

The Dresses by MESSRS. NATHAN, *of Titchbourne Street, Haymarket, and* MISS WILKINS, *of Carburton Street, Fitzroy Square.*
Perruquier, MR. WILSON, *of the Strand.*

CAPTAIN EBSWORTH, *of The Sea Mew*	MR. EDWARD PIGOTT.
CAPTAIN HELDING, *of The Wanderer*	MR. ALFRED DICKENS.
LIEUTENANT CRAYFORD	MR. MARK LEMON.
FRANK ALDERSLEY	MR. WILKIE COLLINS.
RICHARD WARDOUR	MR. CHARLES DICKENS.
LIEUTENANT STEVENTON	MR. YOUNG CHARLES.
JOHN WANT, *Ship's Cook*	MR. AUGUSTUS EGG.
BATESON } *Two of The Sea Mew's People*	{ MR. SHIRLEY BROOKS.
DARKER }	{ MR. FREDERICK EVANS.

(OFFICERS AND CREWS OF THE SEA MEW AND WANDERER.)

MRS. STEVENTON	MISS HELEN.
ROSE EBSWORTH	MISS KATE.
LUCY CRAYFORD	MISS HOGARTH.
CLARA BURNHAM	MISS MARY.
NURSE ESTHER	MRS. FRANCIS.
MAID	MISS MARLEY.

THE SCENERY AND SCENIC EFFECTS OF THE FIRST ACT, BY MR. TELBIN.
THE SCENERY AND SCENIC EFFECTS OF THE SECOND AND THIRD ACTS, BY **Mr. STANFIELD, R.A.**
ASSISTED BY MR. DANSON.
THE ACT DROP, ALSO BY **Mr. STANFIELD, R.A.**

To Conclude with the Farce, in Two Acts,

UNCLE JOHN.

NEPHEW HAWK	MR. WILKIE COLLINS.
EDWARD EASEL	MR. FREDERICK EVANS.
UNCLE JOHN	MR. CHARLES DICKENS.
FRIEND THOMAS	MR. MARK LEMON.
ANDREW	MR. YOUNG CHARLES.
NIECE HAWK	MISS HOGARTH.
ELIZA	MISS KATE.
MRS. COMFORT	MISS MARY.

TERMINATING WITH A DANCE BY THE CHARACTERS.

Musical Composer and Conductor of the Orchestra, Mr. FRANCESCO BERGER,
WHO WILL PRESIDE AT THE PIANO.

The Audience are respectfully desired to be in their places by Ten minutes to 8 o'clock.

STALLS, ONE GUINEA. AREA, TEN SHILLINGS AND SIXPENCE. AMPHITHEATRE, FIVE SHILLINGS.
Tickets for Stalls, Area, and Amphitheatre, to be had at the Committee's Office, Gallery of Illustration, Regent Street, every day from 12 to 4.

REFRESHMENTS.—The Audience are respectfully informed that the Committee have made arrangements with **Mr. RICHARD GUNTER** to supply, during the evening, Tea, Coffee, Cream and Water Ices, Lemonade, Soda Water, &c., &c., at the same Prices as those charged at his Establishment in Motcombe Street.
The Overture to the FROZEN DEEP, composed by Mr. Francesco Berger, is published by Messrs. Ewer & Co., and can be had in the room.

Gallery of Illustration, Regent Street, Playbill for *The Frozen Deep*, by
Wilkie Collins, August 8, 1857.

W.TELBIN -EVANS SHIRLEY BROOKS MᴬᴸᴱMON JUN W.JONES F EVANS MARCUS STONE F.BERGER MARK LEMON Aug EGG COPYRIGHT
ALBERT SMITH G.C.STANFIELD MISS EVANS -PIGOTT   MRS FRANCIS   -LUARD
-KEITH   CHAS DICKENS JUN KATE DICKENS MISS HOGARTH MARY DICKENS WILKIE COLLINS MISS H.HOGARTH
                        CHARLES DICKENS

THE AMATURE COMPANY WHICH PERFORMED 'THE FROZEN DEEP', 1857.

To be had in the Refreshment Room,

THE OVERTURE TO "THE FROZEN DEEP,"

COMPOSED BY FRANCESCO BERGER,

and arranged for the PIANO, SOLO.

Published for the Committee in remembrance of the late

Mr. DOUGLAS JERROLD.

After the death of Douglas Jerrold, playwright and a chief contributor to *Punch*, Dickens organized a series of performances for the benefit of his friend's family. *The Frozen Deep* was staged several times in London and then in Manchester. An overture and incidental music were composed by Francesco Berger, a German musician, whom Charles Dickens, Jr. had met in Leipzig.

"At the time of the Douglas Jerrold performances, in 1857, a special evening was arranged for the Queen to see the acting, and, when it was over, her Majesty sent a message requesting that Dickens would come forward to receive her thanks."

(John Forster, *Forster's Life of Dickens. Abridged and revised by George Gissing.*)

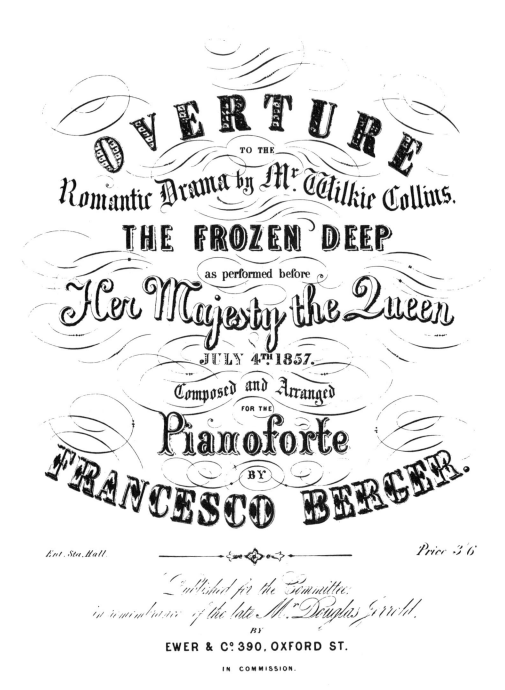

On November 10, 1859, a set of Charles Dickens's *Works*, in the special half morocco crimson binding the author reserved for himself and his special friends, was sent to Wilkie Collins with the message: "This set of the Library Edition of my books, with affectionate regard. In remembrance of The Lighthouse, The Frozen Deep, and much more.' In 1860 Kate Macready ("Katey") Dickens married Charles Allston Collins, Wilkie Collins's brother, a painter whose paintings had been hung on the walls of the Academy in 1852. On June 14th, 1870, when a plain coffin bearing Dickens from Gad's Hill to London was accompanied by three coaches with members of the family, Wilkie Collins, who had shared so much triumph, sat in the third coach with his brother to share the mourning.

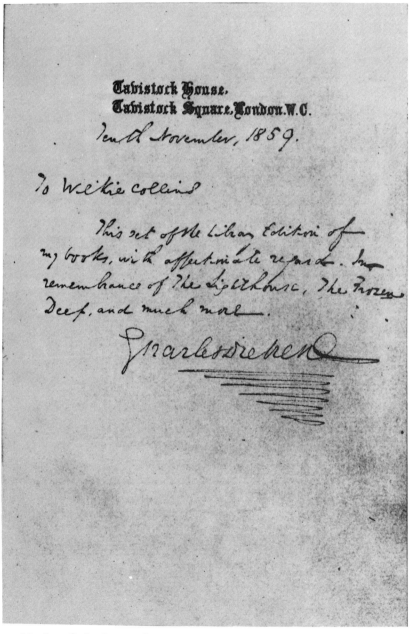

Works of Charles Dickens. Library Edition. 22 vols. London, Chapman and Hall, 1858.

Letter to John Thompson, Gad's Hill Place, August 13, 1857.

Gad's Hill Place
Thursday Thirteenth August
1857

John.

Mr Berger wishes you to take the Bell that is struck in the Frozen Deep, to Manchester, among the properties. (It was left in the Orchestra). My little handbell must be strongly mended, or a new one bought. The clapper always comes out of it, when I want it most.

See that the Snow you take to Manchester, is better made than the last. It was very badly cut, and much too large.

CD

The correspondent to whom this letter is addressed was Dickens's butler. Some time later, he was discharged for theft.

"On the strip of highest ground on the mainroad between Rochester and Gravesend, stood the house called Gadshill-place. Upon first seeing it when in company with his father, and looking up at it with much admiration, Charles had been promised that he himself might live in it or in some such house when he came to be a man, if he would only work hard enough."

(John Forster, *Forster's Life of Dickens. Abridged and revised by George Gissing.*)

On March 14, 1856, Dickens paid the purchase price for his last home Gad's Hill Place, of which he took possession in February, 1857.

Charles Dickens's House at Gad's Hill Place

"I see Barsad, and Cly, Defarge, The Vengeance, the Juryman, the Judge, long ranks of the new oppressors who have risen on the destruction of the old, perishing by this retributive instrument, before it shall cease out of its present use. I see a beautiful city and a brilliant people rising from this abyss, and, in their struggles to be truly free, in their triumphs and defeats, through long years to come, I see the evil of this time and of the previous time of which this is the natural birth, gradually making expiation for itself and wearing out."

(*A Tale of Two Cities*, Book III, Chapter XV.)

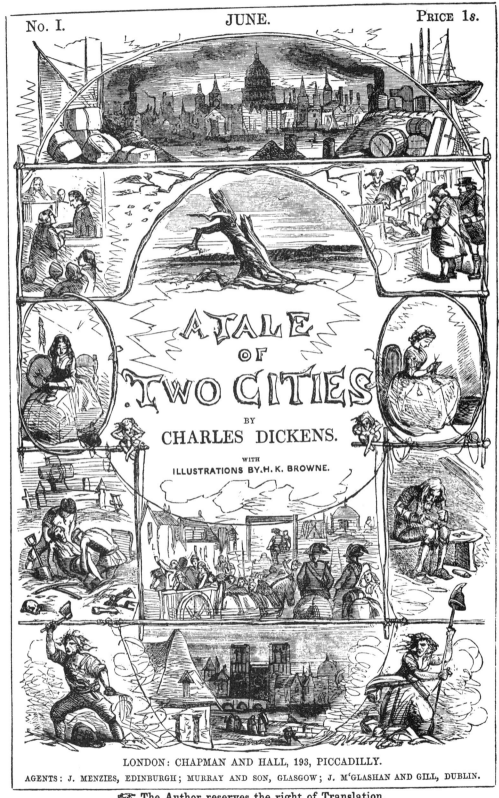

A Tale of Two Cities. No. 1, June [1859]-No. 7-8, December [1859].
London, Chapman and Hall. The first number is illustrated here.

"When I was acting, with my children and friends, in Mr. Wilkie Collins's drama of The Frozen Deep, I first conceived the main idea of this story," wrote Dickens in the "Preface." Dickens discontinued his relationship with Bradbury and Evans, and began his new novel in the first issue of his periodical, *All The Year Round*, published by Chapman and Hall. The time and theme had been his historical favorite for many years, and he knew Carlyle's "wonderful book," the *French Revolution*, intimately. Their theme was alike, that certain conditions lead to anarchy and anarchy destroys itself.

Hablôt K. Browne ("Phiz"). "The Sea Rises." Original pencil drawing for *A Tale of Two Cities*.

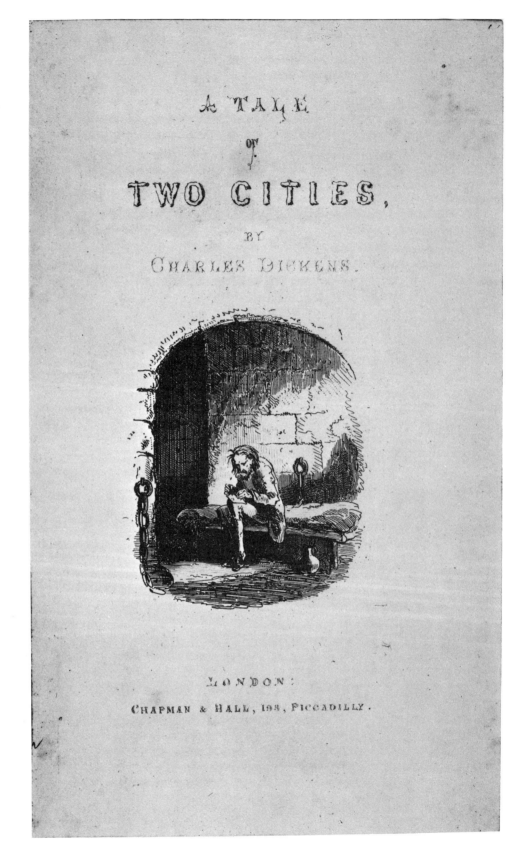

A Tale of Two Cities. London, Chapman and Hall, 1859.

This copy was bound for Dickens, without the illustrations. With his bookplate.

GREET EXPECTATIONS.

———◆———

CHAPTER I.

My father's family name being Pirrip, and my christian name Philip, my infant tongue could make of both names nothing longer or more explicit than Pip. So, I called myself Pip, and came to be called Pip.

I give Pirrip as my father's family name, on the authority of his tombstone and my sister—Mrs. Joe Gargery, who married the blacksmith. As I never saw my father or my mother, and never saw any likeness of either of them (for their days were long before the days of photographs), my first fancies regarding what they were like, were

VOL. I.　　　　　B

Great Expectations. London, Chapman and Hall, 1861.

"From the collector's standpoint, Great Expectations is a most notable and important book, owing to the extreme difficulty in obtaining clean uncut copies in the original cloth . . . Dickens's All the Year Round, towards the end of 1860, had reached a critical state in its career and he came to the decision to bolster its fallen fortunes with one of his own stories. Publication began December 1, 1860, and ended August 3 of the following year. He was deterred from publishing in the monthly parts on account of the ill-success met by A Tale of Two Cities, consequently a three-volume form was decided upon, and so it was issued about the end of June, 1861."

(John C. Eckel, The First Editions of the Writings of Charles Dickens.)

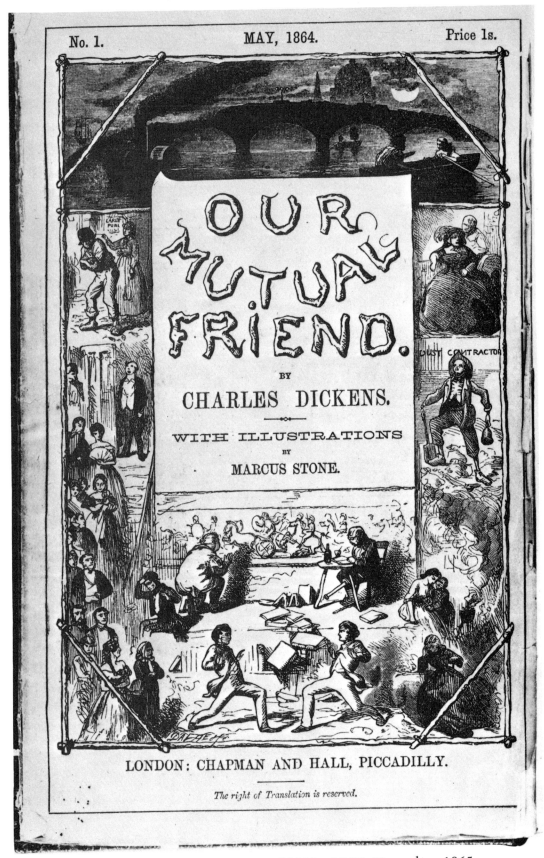

Our Mutual Friend. No. 1, May, 1864-No. 19-20, November, 1865.
London, Chapman and Hall. The first number is illustrated here.

One of Marcus Stone's original ink and wash drawings for *Our Mutual Friend*.

Marcus Stone, then a young artist in his twenties, was asked to do the illustrations. As was his habit, Dickens kept a close watch and "bombarded" his collaborator with instructions.

The Berg Collection has a noteworthy copy of the novel, containing the 40 original drawings, 12 with captions by Dickens, 5 partial sketches of figures, proofs on India paper, the original sketch for the wrappers and the India proof of what was the final illustration for the wrappers.

" 'For I aint, you must know,' said Betty, 'much of a hand at reading writing-hand, though I can read my Bible and most print. And I do love a newspaper. You mightn't think it, but Sloppy is a beautiful reader of a newspaper. He do the Police in different voices.' "

(*Our Mutual Friend*, Book I, Chapter XVI.)

Signatures to the original agreement with Edward and Frederic Chapman for the publication of *Our Mutual Friend*, November 21, 1863.

The firm of Chapman and Hall had witnessed changes and personal losses. William Hall was dead and Edward Chapman was thinking of retirement. His cousin Frederic, now a partner, was bent on giving Dickens anything he wanted.

Our Mutual Friend was the last completed novel Dickens wrote. On June 9, 1865, while Dickens was part of a "terribly destructive accident," a portion of the manuscript was in the railway carriage from which he escaped shaken but unhurt. He climbed back into the carriage to "extricate" his work "much soiled, but otherwise unhurt."

"This is a confoundedly out-of-the-way place," said Mortimer, slipping over the stones and refuse on the shore, as the boy turned the corner sharp.

"Seems so to you, sir, I dare say. They ground here sometimes, when the wind suits the tide."

"Who ground? What ground?"

"This is my father's, sir; where the light is."

The low building had the look of having once been a mill. There was a rotten waste of wood upon its forehead that seemed to indicate where the sails had been; but the whole was very indistinctly seen in the obscurity of the night. The boy lifted the latch of the door, and they passed at once into a low circular room, where a man stood before a red fire, looking down into it; and a girl sat engaged in some rough needlework. The fire was in a rusty brazier, not fitted to the hearth; and a common lamp, shaped like a hyacinth-root, smoked and flared in the neck of a stone bottle on the table. There was a wooden bunk or berth in a corner, and in another corner a wooden stair leading above; so clumsy and steep that it was little better than a ladder. Two or three old sculls and oars stood against the wall, and against another part of the wall was a small dresser, making a spare show of the commonest articles of crockery and cooking-vessels. The roof of the room was not plastered, but was formed of the flooring of the room above. This, being very old, knotted, and beamed, gave a lowering aspect to the chamber; and roof, and walls, and floor, alike abounding in old smears of flour, red-lead (or some such stain which it had probably acquired in warehousing), and damp, alike had a look of decomposition.

"The gentleman, father."

The figure at the red fire turned, raised its ruffled head, and looked like a bird of prey.

"You're Mortimer Lightwood, esquire; are you, sir?"

"Mortimer Lightwood is my name."

"Mine, if it signifies anything to you to know, and in case my son mayn't have mentioned it, is Hexam. I am know'd as Gaffer, but was giv' the lawful name of Jesse. This here is my daughter, Lizzie. This here, as you are aweer, I s'pose, is my son; and this here,"—raising his ruffled head, and casting his eagle eyes around him—"is my perch."

"—What you found," said Mortimer, glancing rather shrinkingly towards the bunk; "is it here?"

"'Tain't not to say here; but it's close by. I do everything reg'lar. I've giv' notice of the circumstance to the police, and the police have took possession of it. No time ain't been lost on any hand. The police have put it into print already, and here's what the print says of it."

Taking up the bottle with the lamp in it, he held it near a paper on the wall, with the police heading, FOUND DROWNED. The two friends read the handbill as it stuck against the wall, and Gaffer read them as he held the light.

"Only papers on the unfortunate man, I see," said Lightwood, glancing from the description of what was found, to the finder.

C

Our Mutual Friend. Proofs of the serial edition, with Dickens's manuscript corrections and in his library binding.

"*Our Mutual Friend* is *The Waste Land* of Dickens's work. Like that poem, it resorts to the realm of myth, and 'for the source of emotional vitality,' as Robert Morse points out, 'draws upon the deepest mythology of mankind.' ...As in the world of Eliot's poem, this London is a waste land of stony rubbish and broken images, of dead trees, dry rock and dust."

(Edgar Johnson, *Charles Dickens.*)

When Edgar Johnson published this commentary in 1952, he did not know that T. S. Eliot, a great admirer of Charles Dickens, used in the manuscript of *The Waste Land*, but later discarded, a line from *Our Mutual Friend*: "He do the Police in different voices."

On November 9, 1867, Dickens set out for America again, and arrived in Boston on the 19th. George Dolby, his lecture manager, had come ahead. Old friends, and new, his American publishers, Howard Ticknor, James T. Fields, and their junior partner James Osgood, joined Dolby in the welcome. From Boston Dickens went to New York and dragged an aching foot and a cold along. His reading schedule would have been excruciating even for a younger man.

On April 21, 1868, the night before Dickens was to sail, Fields told him he felt like erecting a statue to him for heroism in doing his duty. "No, don't," Dickens gasped, laughing at the same time; "take down one of the old ones instead!"

Letter to Mr. Schlesinger, Philadelphia, February 14, 1868.

> *Philadelphia. Fourteenth February*
> *1868*

My Dear Mr Schlesinger.
I am afraid it is absolutely impossible that I can have the pleasure of dining with you at Boston, for want of a single free day. But I propose a treaty. Come and dine with me at the Parker House on Saturday the 29th instead. You will meet some pleasant company, and the occasion is a facetious 12 mile walking match between Messrs Osgood and Dolby.
> *Faithfully Yours*
> *Charles Dickens*

Letter to James T. Fields, Boston, February 27, 1868.

> *Boston, Thursday Ev[enin]g*
> *Twenty Seventh Feb^y*
> *1868.*

My Dear Fields
Dolby will tell you that I have been terrifying him nearly out of his wits by setting in for a paroxysm of sneezing, since dinner. It would be madness in me, with such a cold, and such a night, and with tomorrow's reading before me, to go out after to night's Reading. I have charged Dolby with a little note to Longfellow, explaining. If you want to go home, <u>don't wait to come round to me</u>. But I need not add that I shall be heartily glad to see you if you have time.
> *Ever affectionately*
> *CD*

Already in January in New York Dickens complained about his cold. On February 27th Dickens read the *Christmas Carol*. "They took it so tremendously last night that I was stopped every five minutes. One poor young girl in mourning burst into a passion of grief about Tiny Tim, and was taken out."

Letter to William F. De Cerjat, Gad's Hill Place, January 4, 1869.

Gad's Hill Place, Higham, by Rochester
Monday Fourth January 1869

My Dear Cerjat.

I will answer your question first. Have I done with my Farewell Readings? Lord bless you, No; and I shall think myself well out of it, if I get done by the end of May. I have undertaken 103, and have as yet vanquished only 28. Tomorrow night, I read in London, for the first time, the Murder from Oliver Twist which I have re-arranged for the purpose. Next day I start for Dublin and Belfast; I am just back from Scotland for a few Christmas holidays; I go back there next month; and in the meantime and afterwards go everywhere else.

Take my guarantee for it, — you may be quite comfortable on the subject of Papal aspirations and encroachments. The English people are in unconquerable opposition to that church. They have the animosity in their blood — derived from the history of the past, though perhaps unconsciously. But they do sincerely want to win Ireland over, if they can. They know that since the Union she has been hardly used. They know that Scotland has <u>her</u> religion, and a very uncomfortable one. They know that Scotland though intensely anti-Papal, perceives it to be unjust that Ireland has not <u>her</u> religion too, and has very emphatically declared her opinion in the late Elections. They know that a richly endowed church, forced upon a people who don't belong to it, is a grievance with those people. They know that many things — but especially an artfully and schemingly managed Institution like the Romish church — thrive upon a grievance and that Rome has thriven exceedingly upon this, and made the most of it. Lastly the best among them know that there is a gathering cloud in the West, considerably bigger than a man's hand, under which a powerful Irish-American body, rich and active, is always drawing Ireland in that direction. And that these are not times in which other Powers would back one holding Ireland by force unless we could make our claim good in proving fair and equal government.

Poor Townshend charged me in his will "to publish without alteration, his religious opinions: which he sincerely believes would tend to the happiness of mankind." To publish them without alteration, is absolutely impossible; for they are distributed in the strangest fragments through the strangest note books, pocket books, clips of paper, and what not, and produce a most incoherent and tautological result. I infer that he must have held some always-postponed idea of fitting them together. For which reason I would certainly publish nothing about them, if I had any discretion in the matter. Having none, I suppose a book must be made of them. The claim of the Canton de Vaud on his estate is, I believe, not yet settled. His pictures and rings have gone to the South Kensington Museum, and are now exhibiting there.

Charley Collins is no better, and no worse. He can eat well, and that is about the only sign of a natural or healthy condition that can be detected in him. His wife looks very young and very pretty. Her sister and Miss Hogarth (my joint housekeepers) have been on duty this Christmas, and have had enough to do. My boys are now all dispersed in South America, India, and Australia: except Charley, whom I have taken on at "All The Year Round" office, on his making a sad mess of paper making: and Harry, who is an under Graduate at Trinity Hall, and I hope will make his mark there, all well.

The Thames embankment is (faults of ugliness in detail, apart) the finest public work yet done. From Westminster Bridge to near Waterloo it is now lighted up at night, and has a fine effect. They have begun to plant it with trees; and the footway (not the road) is already open to the Temple. Besides its beauty and its usefulness in relieving the crowded streets, it will greatly quicken and deepen what is learnedly called the "scour" of the river. But the Corporation of London, and some other nuisances have brought the weirs above Twickenham into a very bad and unsound condition; and they already begin to give, and vanish, as the stream runs faster and stronger.

Your undersigned friend has had a few occasional reminders of his "true American Catarrh." My Doctor is of opinion that the disorder in question originates in vegetable poison; and has attacked it with strong and sudden doses of quinine in hot brandy and water. They have been remarkably effectual. Although I have exerted my voice very much, it has not yet been once touched. In America I was obliged to patch it up constantly.

I like to read your Patriarchal account of yourself among your Swiss vines and figtrees. You wouldn't recognize Gads Hill now; I have so changed it, and bought land about it. And yet I often think that if Mary were to marry (which she won't), I should sell it, and go genteelly vagabonding over the face of the Earth. Then indeed I might see Lausanne again. — But I don't seem in the way of it at present; for the older I get, the more I do, and the harder I work.

Take my best wishes, my dear Cerjat for many happy years to you and all who are nearest and dearest to you, and always think of me as

Your affectionate Friend
Charles Dickens

Until March 15, 1870, Dickens kept up his reading schedule. "The Murder from Oliver Twist" was a piece he read over and over again. The author's Swiss friend, Monsieur De Cerjat, companion of his days in Lausanne, was not given much of a hint, other than the "true American Catarrh," that Dickens was in poor health. Yet, there were other, and more serious, symptoms. In April, 1869, it was cautiously noted by his physician that his patient "had been on the brink of an attack of paralysis of his left side, and possibly of apoplexy." In May Dickens made his will.

Letter to Thomas Adolphus Trollope, Office of *All the Year Round*, London, November 4, 1869.

No. 26, Wellington Street, Strand, London,
Thursday Fourth November 1869

My Dear Trollope.

The money had been paid in to your bankers (as I settled with Fanny when she was here) before I received your letter accompanying your pretty story.

I am in the hopeless difficulty concerning the latter that I have already two serial stories accepted and partly printed (for publication in the end of the N^{os}: not the beginning), and consequently have no room for still another serial. Two progressing stories at a time are as much as the small space at command will bear; and I stand pledged to Veronica's successor, as well as to the writers — one after the other — of these two shorter tales.

Moreover: with the utmost care, it is sometimes impossible to prevent a topic from overrunning a single article; and in that case I am driven to all sorts of expedients for renewing it without seeming to distract the reader with still another continuation. This cramps me still more in the arrangement of the (only) four and twenty weekly pages.

I go into these details to explain to you that I am, for some time, at a deadlock as to stories to be continued. What shall I do? Shall I send your MS to you — or to any one — or shall I keep it by me? It shall safely abide your reply at your convenience.

Walk across the Alps? Lord bless you, I am "going" to take up my alpenstock and cross all the Passes, and I am "going" to Italy; I am also "going" up the Nile to the Second Cataract, and I am "going" to Jerusalem, and to India, and likewise to Australia. My only dimness of perception in this wise is that I don't know when. If I did but know when, I should be so wonderfully clear about it all! At present I can't see even so much as the Simplon, in consequence of certain Farewell Readings, and a certain new book (just begun) interposing their dwarfish shadow. But whenever (if ever) I change "going" into "coming", I shall come to see you.

With kind regard
Ever My Dear Trollope
Your affectionate Friend
Charles Dickens

Here's a state of things about Dr Temple of Rugby! Here's a state of things about priesthood generally! Of course you are going (and probably on your knees) to the Council at Rome.

Thomas Adolphus Trollope was the son of Thomas Anthony and Frances Trollope and an author in his own right. A resident in Italy, he could easily invite Dickens to Florence, where he and his wife lived in the "Villino Trollope." In 1873 they moved to Rome - not on their knees.

Letter to B. H. Ticknor, London, February 14, 1870.

5 Hyde Park Place. W.
Monday Fourteenth February
1870

My Dear Sir

I have waited for your return from Paris before answering your letter. I shall be at the office of All The Year Round, 26 Wellington Street Strand, on Wednesday from 12 to 2, and shall be happy to see you there if it will suit your convenience.

Faithfully Yours
Charles Dickens

Because of his dislike of railway travel Dickens rented a house in London at the beginning of 1870. He had become a tenant at 5, Hyde Park Place.

This letter is inserted in a copy of *The Uncommercial Traveller*, 1866, with the running heads revised by Dickens for a later, possibly American, edition. The volume of sketches and much autobiographical material first appeared in seventeen papers in *All the Year Round* and was issued in book form in 1860.

Letter to Chapman and Hall, [London] May 7, 1870.

5 Hyde Park Place W
Saturday Night Seventh May
1870

My Dear Sirs

I return you the sheets of The Child's History for press.

I beg you to be so good as [to] send this note on to Messrs Virtue and C^os reader, in order that I may expressly thank him for his great care and attention. I have observed all his notes, and have found them all perfectly correct: with the exception that he has not borne in mind that the double-spelling of Agincourt and Azincourt is explained in the text. It is there stated (when the battle is described) that the latter was the French name, but that our English historians changed it into the former. I accordingly use the former, ever afterwards.

I am sincerely sensible of the Reader's pains, and am truly obliged to him.

Faithfully Yours always
Charles Dickens

"When I went alone to the Railway to catch my train at night . . . I was in a more charitable mood with Dullborough than I had been all day; and yet in my heart I had loved it all day too! Ah! who was I that I should quarrel with the town for being changed to me, when I myself had come back, so changed, to it! All my early readings and early imaginations dated from this place, and I took them away so full of innocent construction and guileless belief, and I brought them back so worn and torn, so much the wiser and so much the worse!"

(*The Uncommercial Traveller*, "Dullborough Town.")

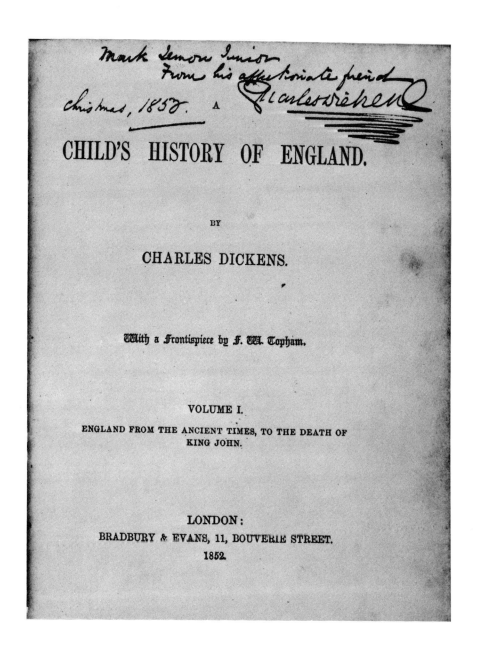

A
CHILD'S HISTORY OF ENGLAND.

BY

CHARLES DICKENS.

With a Frontispiece by F. W. Topham.

VOLUME I.

ENGLAND FROM THE ANCIENT TIMES, TO THE DEATH OF
KING JOHN.

LONDON:
BRADBURY & EVANS, 11, BOUVERIE STREET.
1852.

A Child's History of England. London, Bradbury & Evans,
1852-1854.

Printed first as a serial in *Household Words,* this unfinished story which
Dickens dictated to Georgina Hogarth for the benefit of his son, Charles,
never "quite hit the mark." In 1853 Mark Lemon Junior received from
the author an inscribed copy for Christmas. A month before he died,
Dickens read proofs of this book for the 'Charles Dickens Edition' published by Chapman and Hall from 1867 to 1874.

Portrait of Charles Dickens by an unidentified artist. *ca.* 1869.
Original pencil, dry brush and crayon, heightened with white.

No. VI.]   SEPTEMBER, 1870.   [Price Eighteenpence.

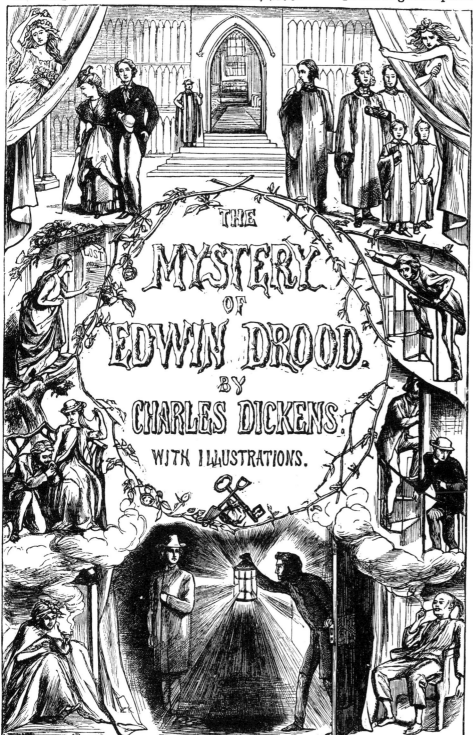

THE MYSTERY OF EDWIN DROOD.

BY CHARLES DICKENS.

WITH ILLUSTRATIONS.

LONDON: CHAPMAN & HALL, 193, PICCADILLY.

Advertisements to be sent to the Publishers, and ADAMS & FRANCIS, 59, Fleet Street, E.C.

[The right of Translation is reserved.]

For three months after his death, Dickens's last story continued in the vein he had planned it. Cloisterham of the story is still the Rochester Dickens loved, but "all its atmosphere is sunset and autumnal." The poetic and mournful tone led Longfellow to feel that *Edwin Drood* was "certainly one of the most beautiful of his works, if not the most beautiful of all."

The Mystery of Edwin Drood. No. 1, April, 1870-No. 6, September, 1870. London, Chapman and Hall. The last number is illustrated here.

SERMON

PREACHED BY

ARTHUR PENRHYN STANLEY, D.D.

DEAN OF WESTMINSTER

In Westminster Abbey

JUNE 19, 1870

(THE FIRST SUNDAY AFTER TRINITY)

BEING THE SUNDAY FOLLOWING

THE FUNERAL OF CHARLES DICKENS

London

MACMILLAN AND CO.

1870

"... But even thus, and even in this sacred place, it is good to remember that, in the writings of him who is gone, we have had the most convincing proof that it is possible to have moved old and young to inextinguishable laughter without the use of a single expression which could defile the purest, or shock the most sensitive. Remember this, if there be any who think that you cannot be witty without being wicked — who think that in order to amuse the world and awaken the interest of hearers or readers, you must descend to filthy jests, and unclean suggestions, and debasing scenes. So may have thought some gifted novelists of former times; but so thought not, so wrote not (to speak only of the departed) Walter Scott, or Jane Austen, or Elizabeth Gaskell, or William Thackeray: so thought not, and so wrote not, the genial and loving humourist whom we now mourn. How deep into the dregs of society his varied imagination led him in his writings to descend, it still breathed an untainted atmosphere. He was able to show us, by his own example, that even in dealing with the darkest scenes and the most degraded characters, genius could be clean, and mirth could be innocent ..."

Extract from the Sermon preached by Dean Stanley
on June 19, 1870.

The Grave of Charles Dickens
Poets' Corner, Westminster Abbey

ACKNOWLEDGMENTS

035818

The compiler of this selection is grateful to Mr. Christopher C. Dickens for his kind permission to publish twenty-three unpublished letters by Charles Dickens and one by John Dickens; to The Clarendon Press for permission to reprint thirty-four letters included in *The Letters of Charles Dickens* (The Pilgrim Edition), volumes 1 (1965) and 2 (1969); to The Nonesuch Press for permission to reprint eight letters included in the Nonesuch Dickens *Letters of Charles Dickens*, volumes 1 to 3 (1938); to Longmans, Green & Company for permission to reprint a quotation from Professor K. J. Fielding's *Charles Dickens: A Critical Introduction* (1965); and to Professor Edgar Johnson for permission to reprint quotations from his *Charles Dickens; His Tragedy and Triumph* (Simon & Schuster 1952), the biography to which all Dickens scholars pay unqualified tribute.

All books have in their history a person or persons "without whom it could not have been possible." To those two in this instance, Philip Kelley and Ronald Hudson, the compiler expresses in print the innumerable thanks expressed while they designed and produced this book.